Delusions in Context

Lisa Bortolotti
Editor

Delusions in Context

palgrave
macmillan

Editor
Lisa Bortolotti
Philosophy Department and Institute for Mental Health
University of Birmingham
Birmingham, UK

This book is an open access publication.
ISBN 978-3-319-97201-5 ISBN 978-3-319-97202-2 (eBook)
https://doi.org/10.1007/978-3-319-97202-2

Library of Congress Control Number: 2018952069

This Palgrave Macmillan imprint is published by the registered company Springer Nature Switzerland AG
The registered company address is: Gewerbestrasse 11, 6330 Cham, Switzerland

Preface

This book gathers some influential views about the relationship between delusional and non-delusional beliefs, and seeks to provide the resources for a better understanding of delusions by considering the clinical, psychological, philosophical, social, and cultural context in which delusional beliefs are adopted and maintained.

The views defended in the four self-standing chapters comprising this book come from experts in different disciplinary areas and reflect a variety of perspectives on the study of delusions and mental health in general, encompassing lived experience, psychology, philosophy, and cognitive neuropsychiatry. The contributors powerfully converge in describing delusions as beliefs that share some of their characteristics with non-delusional beliefs, all the while acknowledging that the concept *belief* needs to undergo some significant revision in order to capture the relevant features of human psychology. Notwithstanding some differences in emphasis, Rachel Upthegrove, Richard Bentall, Philip Corlett, and I commit to the thesis that there is significant continuity between delusional and non-delusional beliefs, and defend the importance of examining delusions in the context in which they emerge.

One thought that echoes in the four chapters is that, for all the effort that has been made in providing a satisfactory definition of delusion, key features of delusions can be found in many beliefs that we do not usually regard as symptoms of mental distress. There are some examples of this thesis throughout the book. In Chap. 1, Rachel Upthegrove and her co-author S.A. write that "outside of mental illness, beliefs in God, aliens, political ideologies etc. can be equally fixed, if not more so, on less evidence" than delusional beliefs. This is a powerful statement, especially considering that fixity and lack of supporting evidence are regarded both as defining features of delusions and as reasons for regarding delusions as irrational and pathological.

In Chap. 2, Philip Corlett observes that, when faced with a belief, it is not always easy to determine whether it is delusional. "Of every 3 Americans, 2 believe that advertisements contain subliminal messages; 1 in 5 would be afraid to sail through the Bermuda Triangle, a similar ratio expressed interest in joining the Freemasons." The point of the examples Corlett refers to is that conspiracy theories and superstitious thinking also feature fixed beliefs that lack supporting evidence, and yet they are very widespread and not symptomatic of mental distress.

In Chap. 3, Richard Bentall characterises delusions as *master interpretive systems*, a new interesting notion aimed at capturing networks of interrelated beliefs that apply to multiple life domains, are not easily refuted, and become part of our identity. Delusions here are compared to political ideologies and religious beliefs, and a case is made for relying on that comparison between them when tackling delusions as a symptom of mental distress.

Finally, in Chap. 4, I remark how the epistemic features of delusions in terms of ill-groundedness and imperviousness to evidence are common in prejudiced and superstitious beliefs. I focus on the similarities between delusions and optimistically biased beliefs, observing that, despite the shared epistemic faults, delusions are thought to affect psychological well-being *negatively*, whereas optimistically biased beliefs are found to have a variety of *beneficial* effects on functioning.

How can we understand the adoption and maintenance of delusional beliefs? There are two main messages in the book. One is that there are elements of continuity between delusional experiences and many of our everyday experiences, and between delusional and non-delusional beliefs. The other is the irrationality and pathological nature commonly attributed to delusions appear as much less exotic and un-understandable when we consider delusions *in context*, that is, in the context of our emotional and cognitive profiles, our life histories, our other commitments and beliefs, the social and cultural groups to which we belong, and more generally the way in which we learn about, and make sense of, the world around us.

Both messages lie at the core of project PERFECT (Pragmatic and Epistemic Role of Factually Erroneous Cognitions and Thoughts 2014–2019), a five-year project hosted by the University of Birmingham and funded by the European Research Council that I have the privilege to lead. It is thanks to the generous support of PERFECT that I had the opportunity to meet Rachel, Philip, and Richard and exchange some ideas with them, after following and admiring their work for years. The project has also enabled me to take the time to conceive of the present volume as a means of continuing our exchange and inviting others to join the conversation.

I hope you will see *Delusions in Context* as evidence that we need open dialogue and genuine collaboration between experts from different disciplines and with different interests and perspectives in order to turn one of the mind's most fascinating mysteries, the adoption and maintenance of delusional beliefs, into a tractable problem, and help people whose lives are disrupted by delusions along the way.

Birmingham, UK Lisa Bortolotti

Contents

List of Figures

CHAPTER 1

Delusional Beliefs in the Clinical Context

Rachel Upthegrove and S. A.

Abstract Delusional beliefs are key symptoms of mental illness, and physicians over hundreds of years have attempted to understand and offer treatments for patients with such beliefs. In this chapter, the authors will explore the experience of delusional beliefs within the clinical context: i.e. with people who present to mental health services for help. The authors begin with definition of the descriptive psychopathology, prevalence and context in which delusional beliefs occur and their clinical relevance. Delusional beliefs have a core role in distress, depression and risk within

Rachel Upthegrove would like to acknowledge the support, enthusiasm and dedication of staff, patients and carers from the Birmingham Early Intervention Service.

S.A. is a Trainee Clinical Psychologist with lived experience of psychosis. The "Healing Healer"? A Psychologist's Personal Narrative of Psychosis and Early Intervention is published in *Schizophrenia Bulletin*, sbx188, https://doi.org/10.1093/schbul/sbx188.

R. Upthegrove (✉)
Institute for Mental Health, University of Birmingham, Birmingham, UK

Birmingham Early Intervention Service, Birmingham, UK
e-mail: R.Upthegrove@bham.ac.uk

S. A.
Institute for Mental Health, University of Birmingham, Birmingham, UK

L. Bortolotti (ed.), *Delusions in Context*,
https://doi.org/10.1007/978-3-319-97202-2_1

psychosis. Real examples will be used to reflect on both the form delusional beliefs take and their personal content, concluding with treatment options and challenges.

Keywords Delusions • Descriptive psychopathology • Distress • Phenomenology • Treatment options • Suicide

1.1 Why Are Psychiatrists Concerned with the 'Treatment' of Beliefs?

Patients, or at times family members advocating on someone's behalf, present to health services in distress and seeking help. In a direct first person account, S.A. explains her experiences of delusional beliefs with candour:

> It is said that even Mother Teresa doubted her faith, yet her religious beliefs directly influenced her charitable actions. Unlike Mother Teresa, my delusions had no room for doubt. I was convinced there was a "Challenge" which placed me at the centre of an elaborate scheme to test my suitability for university. "The Challenge" consumed my every being. As part of it I believed people were recording every thought and every word I spoke. I believed that food and drink were poisonous, which led me to not eating or drinking for four days. Unlike Mother Teresa, there was no good in my belief systems: only terror, anguish and exhaustion.
>
> I was relieved that medication reduced the intensity of my experiences over time. My delusional beliefs eventually subsided, after which I felt an incredible sense of loss that things I concretely experienced were in fact my mind's creation.
>
> I never want to face the horror of a delusion state again, and fortunately I have received mostly excellent care from psychiatric services. Without treatment, I wouldn't have been able to go back to leading a "normal" life and certainly wouldn't be training as a Clinical Psychologist. My personal and clinical experience makes me believe delusions are distinct from other, more helpful beliefs, and it is inhumane not to offer people evidence-based treatments for them.

S.A.'s direct account captures the immediacy of delusional experience with eloquence and candour, and conveys the clinical need for intervention to alleviate distress, but also the need for action in the face of real physical impact: S.A. had withheld food and fluid for a number of days.

This is not a sustainable situation and medicine has this need for action in response to pain and suffering at its core. In the absence of risk or help seeking, psychiatrists and other doctors are not 'thought police' and could not enforce contact or treatment. This is not to deny the abuse of medicine, and psychiatry as a branch of medicine, in darker periods of history; in Soviet countries in the 20th century amongst other examples. Medicine and psychiatry sit within, and are part of, society. It is our social structure and cultural framework that gives context to what defines what are bizarre versus acceptable beliefs. It is thus very evident that we should never lose help-seeking and alleviation of distress or risk as the cornerstone for a psychiatrist's role in treating delusions.

1.2 Prevalence of Delusional Beliefs

Delusions rarely occur in isolation. The lifetime prevalence of delusional disorder, defined as the presence of delusional beliefs but no other symptoms of psychosis, is around 0.18%, in comparison to 3.78% for all other psychotic disorders (Perälä et al., 2007). This is relevant when discussing the context in which beliefs seen in a clinical setting develop, and are held. Delusions are a core feature of schizophrenia, occurring in around 70%, most commonly with concomitant hallucinations and grouped as "positive symptoms" (Fenton, McGlashan, Victor, & Blyler, 1997). In bipolar disorder, there is less literature charting the occurrence of delusions; similar to the presence of mood symptoms in 'non-affective psychoses' such as schizophrenia, the presence of psychosis in affective disorders at a symptom specific level has not been the major focus of attention. However, our previous work demonstrated that up to 70% of people with bipolar disorder would experience psychotic symptoms (lifetime prevalence) with 65% having delusional beliefs (Upthegrove, Chard, et al., 2015). This occurs mostly within an elevated mood (mania) with mood congruent delusions. In major depressive disorder, delusional beliefs are seen in around 20%, mainly the context of severe psychotic depression. Kelleher et al. have also recently demonstrated psychotic symptoms occurring through the range of 'non-psychotic' disorders, regardless of severity, and in the general population (Kelleher & Cannon, 2011). In DSM-5, "Obsessive-Compulsive and Related Disorders" includes a specific reference to 'delusional insight': whereby the obsessional thought is no longer recognised as erroneous, but held with conviction (APA, 2013). In DSM-V delusional disorder itself now has an exclusion criterion, that symptoms cannot be better explained by obsessive-compulsive disorder or similar disorder presenting with a lack of insight. In young people first presenting with mental health problems, in the first development of mental health disorders, diagnostic uncertainty is prominent. In first episode services, delusions are seen in 70% of patients across affective and non-affective psychosis (Upthegrove et al., 2010). Thus, in classification terms delusional beliefs are now not seen wholly or exclusively indicative of psychosis, and this is novel. Whilst hallucinations have long been recognised to occur in non-psychotic disorders, including epilepsy, personality disorder and post traumatic stress disorder (Pierre, 2010), delusional beliefs were not; as Jaspers wrote "to be mad is to be deluded" (Jaspers, 1997).

Within psychosis delusions usually are seen as one of many symptoms, including hallucinations, disordered thinking, cognitive challenges and changes in mood. In phenomenological terms, when considering a belief or experience and the need to describe it, in and of its own appearance, this is within the content of our own and another's inward concerns: we aim to understand and work with people (Broome, 2013). In psychosis, other positive and affective symptoms will impact the way delusions develop, are conveyed and their personal impact. Bebbington and Freeman recently argue for a transdiagnostic extension of delusions to be explored as an experience in bipolar disorder and delusional disorders as well as in schizophrenia: arguing that symptoms (such as mood disorder and delusions) covary because of a causal interaction between symptoms (Bebbington & Freeman, 2017). This proposal in entirely in keeping with the premise of this chapter; where we aim to lay out an understanding of the clinical importance of delusional beliefs within the context in which they develop.

1.3 Phenomenology of Delusions

Delusions are commonly defined as fixed, false beliefs held with certainty and not in keeping with usual social and cultural context. Delusions have been described as a perverted view on reality, held with unusual conviction, not amenable to logic and with their absurdity or erroneous content easily manifest to others (Oyebode, 2014).

S.A. writes:

> I believed there were microphones ("bugs") in my ears that I could switch on and off. This belief was not even shaken when a doctor looked in my ears and confirmed (surprise, surprise) that there weren't any bugs in there.

Historically, diagnostic weight is given in the distinction between primary delusions, which arise in the absence of other symptoms (a rare occurrence), and secondary delusions, which are secondary to other psychopathology e.g. hallucinations or mood disorder, and are thus understandable in circumstances presented to the individual. For example, a person with mania believing they are a prophet, alternatively with severe depression believing they are guilty for all the evil in the world. The importance is not theoretical, but guides the emphasis of treatment: i.e. focus on the primary cause, in these examples the focus of treatment would be on the mania or depression. In schizophrenia, delusions may be secondary to a range of other positive symptoms (hallucinations, disorganisation) or occur in their primary form:

> Andrew walks in to the clinic, clutching a carrier bag, beaming. Despite his many personal challenges, depression has never been a feature of Andrew's presentation. Today however, he is positively upbeat and clearly desperate to show me what is in the bag. 'I've got it doc, I've got proof! Once you see this you will know I am a psychic'. Andrew produces a slightly dog-eared certificate, issued by one of the growing 24-hour psychic TV channels, certifying that he is a Medium. Andrew has paid £1000 for this, and with further investment he tells me he will be allowed to receive live calls from the public for telepathic readings. Andrew believes that his talents have brought him to the attention of MI5 and the CIA, who are working together to put him through psychic training by 'telepathically torturing' him until an undefined point in the future, when he will have passed their initiation, and become a member of an elite telepathic spy ring. His feels this job on TV will keep him busy until this day, and his destiny is revealed. His beliefs have been firm for nearly 5 years. The torture he experiences takes place by way of the secret services moving various organs in his body, with a considerable amount of perceived pain, and by them inducing sensations in his rectum and bowels of being raped, together with many voices and tactile hallucinations of being punched, touched and at times even tickled.
>
> Like the back pay from his disability benefits payment, Andrew uses his latest piece of evidence to reinforce his beliefs and with a kind, benevolent disposition takes the clinical teams continued non-committed response as a further sign that the conspiracy is indeed well hidden. We are mere pawns in the bigger game.

Andrew believes he is telepathic and this belief is false, and fixed. It could be debated as to whether it is out of keeping with his social and cultural background, as a belief in telepathy will be shared by a number of individuals in modern society. However, Andrew's belief arises secondary to his array of tactile, somatic and auditory hallucinations. He uses extensive and increasing information to reinforce his firm belief and discounts evidence that challenges his conviction.

None of the premises for defining delusions are set in stone (that they are fixed and false beliefs) and each point is are open to challenge. However, the presence, clinical relevance and reality of delusions are not belied by the difficulty in definition. Outside of mental illness, beliefs in God, aliens, political ideologies etc. can be equally fixed, if not more so, on less evidence than Andrew may acquire. Insight may come and go, and with this the fixed nature of delusions. Delusions may not be necessarily false, and occur within a cultural and social context for every individual. Yet despite the readily apparent difficulty in definition, delusions remain a cornerstone of the diagnosis of psychosis and severe mental illness. In asking why psychiatry is so pre-occupied with these erroneous beliefs, it is always important to consider the context within which they arise (i.e. rarely in isolation), but primarily the distress and negative impact they can bring.

1.4 From Jaspers to the Modern Era

Karl Jaspers wrote his *General Psychopathology* in 1913, based on years of detailed clinical assessments of patients with (pharmacologically) untreated mental illness. In describing delusions, Jaspers lays out a two-step process; delusional atmosphere and the crystallisation of this into delusions proper (Jaspers, 1997). Jaspers and then Hagen developed the idea of delusional atmosphere to delusional mood; both authors describing a period of uncertainty, of being aware something is changed:

'Patients feel uncanny, and as though something suspicious is afoot. Everything gets a new meaning. The environment is somehow different – not to a gross degree....' The experience of delusional atmosphere or mood is uncomfortable, and the 'full strength of intelligent personality' is called in to understand the experience. Thus, the *delusion proper* which follows is to some extent a reasoning or resolution of this change (Jaspers, 1997; Stanghellini & Fuchs, 2013).

S.A. writes:

> At an earlier stage of my illness it felt as though the atmosphere of the earth had changed in some way that was difficult to put my finger on. I believe my

later delusions about being analysed and controlled by others arose from this feeling of something being different, and was a way of my brain trying to explain it.

Maj highlights that Jaspers' account of delusional atmosphere was in itself an unpleasant experience, often accompanied by mood symptoms, *'a distrustful, uncanny tension invades... they suffer terribly... no dread is worse than the dread unknown'* (Maj, 2013). The resolution of this uncomfortable atmosphere, delusional belief formation, was seen as a resolution of tension, conflict in thought and experience.

Over a century after Jaspers, the idea of delusional mood has re-emerged, with Kapur's model of aberrant salience, further developed by Mishara and Fusar-Poli (Kapur, 2003; Mishara & Fusar-Poli, 2013). The primary difficulty they propose lies in dopamine firing independent of cue. In usual semantic memory development and retrieval, sub-second awareness of the significance of an environmental stimulus is needed, all the time. However, we lack the time and ability to constantly consciously ascertain the significant signal; e.g. food, to assess the shape, colour, smell etc. Seen once, a tiger will remain threatening in our memory and one will always remember the smell, texture and taste of chocolate. These semantic memories are hard wired, quickly, through a salience dopamine pathway.

There is increasing evidence that in psychosis, increase release and unconnected triggering of dopamine occurs (Murray et al., 2008). This is a much more nuanced understanding than an excess of dopamine leading to psychosis. Dopamine is a key neurochemical for memory and memory retrieval, and is increased at a cellular sub-second threshold when one is confronted with important information (the tiger or chocolate). If this firing happens independent of cue, as is proposed, supposedly neutral objects or pieces of information may assume significance; the environment somehow seems different, benign objects acquire special meaning. Inappropriate salience is assigned to external and internal stimuli; thus, a passing car becomes perplexing, or perceived as a threat, memories become pre-occupying or take on new significance.

More recent meta-analysis have confirmed dopamine dysregulation in psychosis; with the summary of findings being increased dopamine synthesis capacity, dopamine release and synaptic concentrations, the sum result of which is increased availability of dopamine to be present 'independent of cue' (Howes et al., 2012). Furthermore, key dopamine and salience networks in the brain have consistently been shown to be functioning differently in patients with psychosis. We are now aware that the brain changes in psychosis will not be related to one area or region, or on indeed one chemical, however certain brain networks of neuronal connections are increasingly recognised as important in our higher order thinking.

The Salience Network consists of the anterior cingulate cortex and anterior insula and, in health, is involved when our attention is needed- it will activate when we need to attend. The Default Mode Network, consisting of the posterior cingulate, ventromedial prefrontal cortex, inferior parietal cortex and angular gyrus, is active when we are not attending (e.g. day dreaming) and the Central Executive Network is involved in our decisions around what is important to attend to, and processing and responding to the complex information. Individuals with psychosis have structural, functional and neurochemical changes within these three networks and how they activate; Palaniyappan, Mallikarjun and Liddle propose switching is a key difficulty; with default mode downregulation not occurring when it should, leading to inappropriate significance being placed on previously benign signals and delusional interpretation of external or internal cues (Palaniyappan, Mallikarjun, Joseph, White, & Liddle, 2011).

Whilst Jaspers was writing about the phenomenology and subjective patient experiences, of distress, delusional mood and the need for resolution, there is a wealth of information now available that builds on this in our understanding of the context in which delusional beliefs are formed; within the context of a change in brain function. In keeping with the tenant of this chapter, however, it should be noted that these changes are not necessarily specific to delusions over and above other positive symptoms; hallucinations may equally be attributable to dopamine activation independent of cue, with that cue being our own inner speech and salience network dysfunction, or the failure to down regulate the default mode network result internal processes being experienced as heard perceptions (Upthegrove, Ives, et al., 2016). The intricate need for understanding hallucinations and delusions together remains prominent. Primary delusions, the springing to mind of fully formed beliefs, complex and fixed, sometimes preceded by a mood of disquiet (delusional mood), are rarely captured. Current understanding and research in delusional beliefs is largely based on persecutory beliefs, as a continuum approach, or secondary delusions.

1.5 Psychosis Continuum

In the past 20 years, the early identification of psychosis has become a priority, based on the knowledge that a longer duration of untreated psychosis is associated with poorer outcomes, functional decline and risk. In the UK and Australia, Early Intervention in Psychosis (EIP) services have been set up with the aim of early identification of young people with first episode psychosis, and also those at risk of developing psychosis. Criteria for 'Ultra High Risk' (UHR) patients, i.e. those at higher risk of developing psychosis, but not yet psychotic, and the concept of an 'At Risk Mental State' (ARMS) includes at the heart a definition of a psychosis as the presence of positive symptoms, including delusions, and that this psychosis exists in a continuum between normal experience and illness (Marwaha, Thompson, Upthegrove, & Broome, 2016). EIP services often offer support and treatment to individuals who may be at high risk of developing psychosis, before frank illness is present, before positive symptoms including delusions are fully developed. In work by Yung et al. (Yung et al., 2008; Yung et al., 2005), ARMS young people are defined as a help-seeking population with either low grade or frequency psychotic like symptoms, very brief self-resolving periods of delusional like thinking and a family history of psychosis along with functional decline. Low-grade psychotic like symptoms may include unusual thoughts or non-bizarre ideas that are not held with a fixed belief, or if they are, they are brief and limited, resolving without interventions. As a group, their relative risk of developing full psychosis in a 3-year period is around 500 times that of the general population (Nelson et al., 2013).

There remains the need for valid biological markers of a psychosis continuum and the staged model of psychotic illness, to aid accuracy of prediction of future psychosis and staged interventions. However, Reniers and colleagues recently demonstrated a neurobiological signature for poorer functional outcome in the ARMS group, consisting of reduced grey matter density in bilateral frontal and limbic areas, and left cerebellum, which may be more clinically relevant than transition to a predetermined definition of psychosis (Reniers et al., 2017). Structural brain alterations are clearly present in those who have schizophrenia and related psychoses, including increase in ventricular volume and reduced grey and white matter. It has also been shown that these changes are present before the onset phase of frank psychosis (Smieskova et al., 2010). The majority of UHR individuals do not transition to psychosis but many continue to have other poor outcomes and lower functioning (Reniers et al., 2017). However the point here is firstly that it is proposed that delusions may exist on a continuum and that positive symptoms are conceptualized together, frequently co-occurring. Their sum total is more than the individual experience of one in isolation, but may not be the most relevant feature of how one functions in the world.

Cornblatt and colleagues propose a dimension of UHR status that has an underlying vulnerability for positive psychotic symptoms driven to clinical significance by cognitive deficits, mood disturbances, social isolation, and school failure (Cornblatt et al., 2003). An alternative approach to recognizing developing psychosis before frank delusions are present has been proposed within the European tradition of Basic Symptoms. Schultze-Lutter and Ruhrmann developed UHR criteria based on basic symptoms as a complement to attenuated positive symptoms, and this aids predictive validity of psychosis risk (Schultze-Lutter, Ruhrmann, Berning, Maier, & Klosterkötter, 2008). Basic symptoms are subtle, sub-clinical self-experiences such as disturbances in drive, stress tolerance, attention, thinking, speech, perception and motor action. First described by Huber, they are based in the subjective understanding of difference from a 'normal' self (Huber & Gross, 1989). Ruhrmann proposes that basic symptoms are compensated for by increasing effort, not available to observation from others, and are recognized by an individual as a product of their own mind (Schultze-Lutter, Klosterkötter, & Ruhrmann, 2014). With relevance to delusions, cognitive basic symptoms include disturbances in thought processing such as thought blockages, perseveration and pressure. Broome demonstrated individuals at high risk of psychosis were more likely to jump to conclusions (JTC) on the basis of less information when cognitive demands are high (Broome et al., 2007). Subjects at high risk of psychosis and controls completed a bead-jar task, where by decisions on which of two jars with different numbers of coloured beads are made when a varying number of beads are shown. A JTC bias is seen when subjects make a decision about which jar on fewer number of beads. When involved in an additional working memory task, subjects with high levels of delusional like thinking were more likely to show a jumping to conclusions bias. Thus the primary cognitive difficulty or working memory was managed by decision-making at an earlier stage. A subtle compensatory response to basic cognitive disturbance demonstrates that even at the first delusional belief formation stage, the influence of other 'symptoms' or processes are key (Garety & Freeman, 1999).

1.6 Delusions in Context

As illustrated in Andrew's presentation, delusional beliefs in frank psychosis do not occur in isolation, and the understanding of their experience requires appreciation of the wider context. As illustrated in S.A.'s account, for many people delusional beliefs are terrifying, consuming experiences, directly related to depression or severe anxiety. Delusional belief may arise secondary to, or in conjunction with, other symptoms; believing that you are being followed as the result of a voice telling you this happening, believing there are telepathic cameras in the walls because somehow your thoughts are being broadcast on the radio. These beliefs are understandable, and have logic. In Jaspers' view these would be delusion-like ideas, and not 'true' delusions (Oyebode, 2014). It must be emphasised that the historical context of the phrase 'true delusions' or 'delusions proper' did not negate the significance or distress of Jaspers' concept of delusion-like ideas, but underlied that there was significance in the cognitive process and the treatment implications that primary delusions bring.

Delusions and Hallucinations: Positive Symptoms

As rehearsed above, the majority of patients will experience both delusional beliefs and hallucinations together as part of 'positive symptoms' of psychosis. Their experiences are interdependent, and can have a combined significant bidirectional impact on an individual's distress, help seeking behaviour and functioning. When investigating the experience of hallucinations in psychosis, this intricate relationship is clear; how one interprets early hallucinatory experiences, attributes cause and meaning to voice content is significant in psychosis. Delusional interpretation of hallucinations is common, particularly in developing illness.

S.A. remarks:

> I believe that my delusion that the water supply had been contaminated was as a result of the water itself tasting different (i.e. a gustatory hallucination).

In a phenomenological study investigating the subjective experience of voice hearing in 25 young people with first episode psychosis, first person accounts show that hallucinations were characterized by an experience of entity: as though from a living being with complex social interchange and control. Voices were often percived as speaking as an expert authority, able to control individuals, received with passivity and accompanied by sensation in other modalities (Upthegrove, Ives, et al., 2016). Thus, is not surprising that delusional beliefs of communication or possession were a common accompaniment such experiences. Direct quotes from individal experence give illustration below:

> 'it's like being possessed, you know. What can you do? What can you really do?'
> 'it's like I'm being held down'
> 'I'm constantly caged in by voices'
> 'my body will recognise it'
> 'When they choose to talk to me, they choose to talk to me and they take over they take over the whole situation as it is at the time'
> 'it's out of my hands'
> 'if it's really strong, the pull, I just lose whole control of it'

The experience of voice hearing is often accompanied by a search for meaning, an understanding of what can be an unusual and isolating experience; shame, and self-stigma lead to and isolation and can result in individuals not discussing experiences with a trusted other, and searching for meaning on their own;

> 'I don't know what kind of game they're playing but someone's gonna end up getting hurt really bad if they keep it up, whether it's me or them'
> 'there must be a camera in the TV then, I mean I don't give a shit'
> 'Is there a solution, has someone else gone through this, is there information on what I'm going through?'
> 'I've experienced it for a good long time on my own because I was embarrassed by it so I did go internet'
> 'made me think… is this really happening… I mean are these people being watched or something'
> 'that's probably why they're using voices that you recognise from back in the day and it's like "We use these to try to connect"'

Thus in our phenomenological study in first episode psychosis, the experience of auditory hallucinations are much more than a mere auditory phenomenon. In a modern phenomenological investigation, without presupposition, results echo known descriptive psychopathology. Novel findings also emerged that may be features of hallucinations in psychosis not currently captured with standardized measures used to assess voices in research and clinical settings. However the complex, personal and multisensory nature of hallucinations is readily apparent. Hallucinations were received with passivity, and lead to the need to understand this experience, and for some individuals a delusional explanation.

Delusions and Mood

Garety and Freeman have long written on the centrality of mood symptoms (depressionand anxiety) in the maintenance of delusional beliefs. Persecutory delusions can be seen as beliefs of threat, and so share the subjectve experience of an anticipation of danger with anxiety disorders. People with persecutory delusions may act in ways, like those with anxiety disorder, to keep safe, and will thus avoid exposure to dis-confirmatory evidence (Freeman, Garety, & Kuipers, 2001). However we have also shown the common occurrence of depression in developing and early psychosis: and that this may indeed be more than a 'comorbidity' (Upthegrove, Marwaha, & Birchwood, 2016; Upthegrove, Ross, Brunet, McCollum, & Jones, 2014). Depression can be seen as a reaction to the threat posed by perceived persecutors, malevolent voices and engagement in safety behaviours leading to feelings of entrapment. Garety and Freeman's work (Freeman et al., 2001; Freeman et al., 2007) demonstrates the significance of safety behaviours in the development and maintenance of delusional belief and distress. This suggests the personal significance and reaction to perceived threat is more individually important than the severity of symptoms as measured by delusional conviction or voice frequency.

Our work has demonstrated that personal appraisal of anomalous experiences may drive on-going emotional dysfunction and through this further increases in the fixed nature of delusional beliefs. Thwarted escape, arrested flight and failure to exert or win control of symptoms through use of self-help or safety behaviours may drive further isolation, lack of exposure to dis-confirmatory evidence and longer duration of untreated illness (Upthegrove, Marwaha, et al., 2016). Learned helplessness, in response to unrelenting positive symptoms also leads to depression until treatment or help finally arrives. This is in keeping with advances in our understanding of anxiety and distress in psychosis whereby proneness to shame is driven by social anxiety disorder (Kesting & Lincoln, 2013; Rüsch, Angermeyer, & Corrigan, 2005).

Building on the importance of mood symptoms in the development and maintenance of positive symptoms, it is also proposed that the context of adverse experiences in childhood will lead to the development of negative schemas of the self and the world (the self as vulnerable and others as dangerous) which facilitate the development of paranoid delusions (Birchwood et al., 2004; Garety, Kuipers, Fowler, Freeman, & Bebbington, 2001).

S.A. writes:

> The content of my delusions (e.g. being tested to see if I was 'good enough' for university) directly related to what I believed about myself, for instance that I was inferior to other people.

Birchwood and colleagues suggest that childhood experience of social adversity leads to the development of negative schemas involving social humiliation and subordination, which in turn may fuel paranoia (Birchwood et al., 2004). Alternatively, within biological models of schizophrenia the experience of abuse is proposed to create vulnerability to psychosis through heightened stress reactivity and cortisol dysfunction (Cannon, Clarke, & Cotter, 2014; Catone et al., 2015). Etain and colleagues suggest that a dual role of genetic and environmental influences of socially and morally inappropriate rewards and parental attitudes during childhood induces affective dysregulation in the developing child that precedes the development of bipolar disorder (Etain, Henry, Bellivier, Mathieu, & Leboyer, 2008).

We have previously investigated delusions in bipolar disorder, using data from 2019 participants from the Bipolar Disorder Research Network, the largest bipolar sample in the world, with lifetime-ever DSM-IV and lifetime-ever clinical characteristics including childhood trauma, presence/absence of specific delusions (including persecutory, grandiose, depressive, nihilistic, guilt, and reference); auditory hallucinations (including mood congruent hallucinations, accusatory/abusive and running commentary) and visual hallucinations (including all visual and mood congruent visual hallucinations). We hypothesised adverse childhood events would show a significant association with positive symptoms driven by dysregulation of mood (mood congruent delusions and hallucinations) or with a persecutory or abusive content. However, our hypothesis was only partially upheld. We demonstrated significant associations between childhood abuse and hallucinations which are mood congruent, or with an abusive content. These types of hallucinations remained significantly associated with childhood sexual abuse even after controlling for other factors such as cannabis misuse. Significant associations were also found for other types of adverse childhood life events, including the experience of bullying and hallucinations but there was not an increased risk of delusional beliefs, or in any sub type of delusional beliefs, in those with childhood traumas (Upthegrove, Chard et al., 2015).

In this respect, our results were contrary to studies in schizophrenia, or in those sampling from a population based cohort investigating associations between childhood trauma and persecutory ideation. However, the majority of this research concerning childhood adverse experiences and psychosis tend to show childhood emotional and sexual abuse are most notably associated with auditory hallucinations; Daalman and colleagues found that psychotic patients with auditory verbal hallucinations were 3 times more likely to be victims of childhood sexual abuse and over 5 times more likely to have suffered emotional abuse than healthy controls (Daalman et al., 2012). In fact, relatively few studies have shown a direct relationship between childhood trauma and fully formed delusions in clinical samples specifically. It may well be that the relationship between childhood events and psychosis is more symptom-specific than first proposed or that hallucinations are the mediating step between trauma and delusional beliefs. This will have relevance through the whole psychosis spectrum, however the weight of symptoms may differ across an affective load. An alternative explanation may be that in bipolar disorder, where there is less cognitive impairment compared to core schizophrenia, the role of childhood trauma appears specific in the predisposition to hallucinations. Additional cognition inefficiency maybe needed for the pathway to be directly between trauma and delusional beliefs.

However, it is also possible that mood symptoms are intricately linked to delusional beliefs at the biological level. Regions critical to emotional processing are common in models of psychotic symptoms and include the hippocampus, insula and prefrontal cortex. These areas are implicated in both depression with psychosis and schizophrenia (Busatto, 2013). In broader terms of affective instability, there is some convergence of evidence that alterations in amygdala activation is involved in difficulty in emotional processing, salience to emotional stimuli, and behavioural response (Broome, He, Iftikhar, Eyden, & Marwaha, 2015). This may not only explain some of the commonality in biological findings across psychotic mood disorders and schizophrenia, but provides potential aetiological pathways.

Recently we have proposed that mood may drive forward further symptom dimensions in psychosis, including delusional beliefs, through a stress-inflammation-structural brain change pathway. Evidence shows that first episode schizophrenia and first episode affective psychosis have similar changes in brain structure, although progressive insular grey matter loss may be more pronounced in schizophrenia (Lee et al., 2015). Increase in stress reactivity seen in schizophrenia may be linked to inflammatory and structural brain changes (Lataster, Valmaggia, Lardinois, van Os, & Myin-Germeys, 2013). Hippocampal grey matter volume (GMV) reduction is found in unipolar depression, related to the duration of illness (Arnone et al., 2013) but is also seen in schizophrenia. Inflammation mediated effects on brain derived neurotrophic factor (BDNF) is a proposed pathway for this effect (Mondelli et al., 2011). Changes in circulating inflammatory markers and neurotrophins associated with the onset of depression are also seen commonly in schizophrenia (Upthegrove, Manzanares-Teson, & Barnes, 2014); psychosis and depression may in combination be significant at a biological inflammatory level; Noto recently demonstrated that IL-6, IL-4, IL-10 and TNFα were significantly higher in this patient group (Noto et al., 2015).

In brain imaging using functional magnetic resonance imaging (fMRI), patients with depression and positive symptoms show similarly enhanced brain response to fearful facial expressions, particularly located to the thalamus (Kumari et al., 2015). Regions critical to emotional processing are common in models of psychotic symptoms and include the hippocampus, insula and prefrontal cortex and these areas are implicated in both depression with psychosis and schizophrenia (Busatto, 2013). There is also convergence of evidence that alterations in amygdala activation is involved in difficulty in emotional processing, salience to emotional stimuli, and behavioral response as related to affective instability (Broome et al., 2015).

Delusions and PTSD

Around one in three people with psychosis report symptoms consistent with post traumatic stress disorder (PTSD), and this can be related to the experience of positive symptoms themselves. Brunet et al. explored PTSD in relation to symptoms and the experience of psychosis in a community sample of patients with first episode psychosis. 31% met DSM-IV criteria for PTSD (Brunet, Birchwood, Upthegrove, Michail, & Ross, 2012), a figure in keeping with PTSD rates after national disasters, and higher than other man-made or technical incidents (Neria, Nandi, & Galea, 2008). In psychosis, more people still report distressing memories subthreshold for PTSD such that two thirds of people experienced distressing intrusive memories at some level (Brunet et al., 2012). PTSD symptoms were often related to psychotic symptoms, which continued to distress participants longitudinally after their first acute episode. In relation to delusional beliefs, threatening persecutors were distressing. Chisholm et al. previously demonstrated the appraisals of threat or harm arising from these experiences and the accompanying distress was associated with PTSD status and severity and those with PTSD appraised their persecutors as more powerful, awful, deserved, and felt less in control or able to cope (Chisholm, Freeman, & Cooke, 2006).

S.A. writes:

> Once I had recovered from my psychotic episode I struggled with distressing memories of what had happened. I didn't develop full PTSD but can understand why it is so common.

Delusions and Suicidal Thinking

In keeping with the premise the clinical context of this chapter, it is important to rehearse suicidal thinking: a clear consequence of delusional beliefs over and above depression and distress. The intricate relationship between mood and delusions has significant consequence. Suicide in psychotic disorders remains too frequent an event and a tragic, preventable loss of life with widespread impact to family, carers, friends and society. In our previous work in first episode psychosis, over 50% of individuals with psychosis reported clear thoughts of self-harm. 33% reported a lifetime history of suicidal behaviour and 30% had a history of suicidal behaviour in the developing months of first episode psychosis or during a period of untreated positive symptoms. Methods used in this cohort include overdose attempted hanging and jumping from a height (Upthegrove et al., 2010). The presence of depression significantly associated with the presence of acts of self-harm. Our investigation of first episode psychosis identified key variables in prediction of suicidal behaviour including male gender male, minority ethnicity grouping, substance abuse and a history of depression (Upthegrove et al., 2010). As we have previously rehearsed, depression can be experienced as a complex reaction to psychosis, including delusional beliefs and the impact of psychosis, thwarted escape, self stigma and internalised shame contributing to a pathway of suicidal thinking (Fig. 1.1):

We have explored this model with qualitative methods using photo-elicitation, together with unstructured interviews, used to characterise

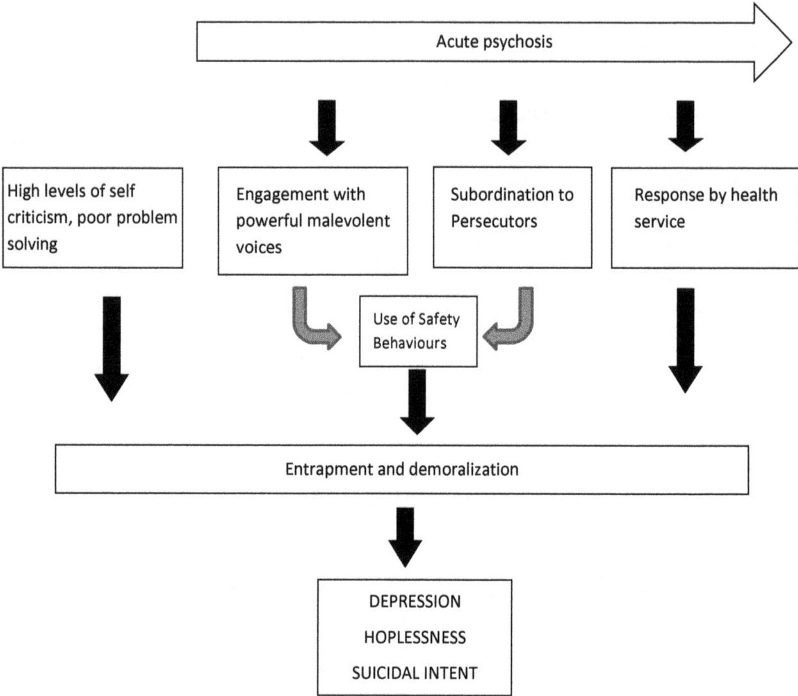

Fig. 1.1 Model of suicidal behaviour in psychosis

aspects of depression following FEP and analysed using contemporary framework analysis. Participants reported a long period of self reflection and an in-depth questioning of their illness events together with a difficulty in trusting their own thoughts and experiences. See Fig. 1.2 and excerpts below from Sandhu et al. (Sandhu, Ives, Birchwood, & Upthegrove, 2013):

> *'That's me describing my mind sometimes, it's kind of like confusion … because after I had a psychosis episode, that's how my mind was like, fully confused, and I couldn't break out of it'.*

Some participants extended the doubt of their thoughts and memories, and raised the possibility that they had been delusional for a much longer period than they originally thought. They also experienced confusion

Fig. 1.2 The participant reported with this illustration *"for a big part of time I was like looking on the internet... trying to understand what's happened to me... there's the part of this experience of 'what's going on?' leads you to try and investigate"*

about the present, and reported an increasing sense of mistrust of both their current thoughts and their current experience of "reality":

> 'I started to realise, if most of the things that I was scared about, and you know, a lot of my thoughts, were they to do with psychosis? ... It's come to the stage where I don't one hundred percent trust myself.'
>
> 'Once you realize that you've lost track of reality and your mind starts getting to grips with the fact that it was wrong, it was completely wrong for so long, I dunno, you kind of lose your confidence in your own judgment'

We also observed an overwhelming sense of shame, which strengthened participants' feelings of loss and social withdrawal. There is substantial evidence that people with mental health disorders, particularly schizophrenia, are heavily subjected to stigma by society and individuals can internalize this stigma and suffer shame, loss of self esteem and isolation (Staring, Van der Gaag, Van den Berge, Duivenvoorden, & Mulder, 2009). Superimposed onto these experiences, our findings suggested an on-going relationship between these disempowering appraisals and fear of psychosis, and the return of delusional thinking adding to loss and isolation. Participants cited feeling safe in isolation, of wanting to be left alone. There was a perceived pressure to 'be better' once positive symptoms had abated; yet with little knowledge about how to begin this, adding to a sense of despair and demoralisation (Sandhu et al., 2013).

Formal comparison between social anxiety disorders and social anxiety in psychosis has recently revealed differing mechanisms involved in maintaining anxiety in patients with psychosis; patients with psychosis experiencing more perceived threat and anticipated harm, without the presence of persecutory delusions. The suggestion is, similar to depression following psychosis, different mechanisms may be involved when affective dysregulation occurs in psychosis (Michail & Birchwood, 2009).

1.7 Therapeutic Options

The first thing to note is that the treatment for delusional beliefs, like their development, does not occur in isolation. Patients present to services with the above rehearsed concomitant distress, hallucinations, depression or suicidal thinking. Therapeutic options are planned with the patient, and their personal formulation, as a whole. On occasion, delusional beliefs singularly come with actions that present significant risk to self or others and this may result in more coercive treatment frameworks, including that involving legislative frameworks. This latter scenario is outside of the scope of this chapter, and would warrant an additional rehearsal of ethical debate and therapeutic challenge. Thus, we will discuss treatment options that mental health professionals; psychiatrists, nurses and psychologists discuss with their help-seeking patient.

That said, risk assessment and management are core features of clinical services. As illustrated above, significant distress, suicidal thinking and actions can accompany delusional beliefs. At times services can struggle with the balance of individual autonomy versus interventions that may save lives, whilst still aiming to offer real clinical hope. The absolute need to engage therapeutically with people in the midst of extraordinary personal experiences are not easily captured or helped by dry definitions of psychopathology, labelling symptoms, establishing diagnostic criteria or an understanding of the underlying neurobiology. In order to offer treatment and interventions, and reduce risk of suicide, there is a need to understand and empathise with an individual's experience - to walk fully in someone else's shoes. This takes time and effort. Therapeutic engagement should be the starting point and continuing cornerstone of pharmacological or psychological treatments, which will not be accepted, or be effective, without.

S.A. writes:

> Before I saw professionals from the Early Intervention Service I didn't feel listened to or understood. My psychiatrist and CPN took time to listen to me and I felt they placed themselves alongside me rather than in a position of power. If they hadn't taken time to get to know me I wouldn't have felt able to trust them or the advice they gave me.

Medication

There is substantial and robust evidence that antipsychotic medication is effective in the treatment of positive symptoms of psychosis (i.e. delusions, hallucinations and disorganisation of thought). The British Association for Psychopharmacology (BAP) guidance summarised evidence that the majority of patients with positive symptoms will respond to antipsychotic medication and recommends that the choice of first-line antipsychotic drug should be based on the evidence for relative liability for side effects, individual patient preference, individual patient risk factors for side effects and relevant medical history. Antipsychotic medication should be initiated at the lower end of the licensed dosage range when first commenced and an individual trial of the antipsychotic of choice should be conducted: i.e. it is not advised, nor responsible, to continue prescription for medication which may have side effects but has not shown a therapeutic benefit. Clozapine should be considered for patients whose illness has shown a poor response to trials of two antipsychotic drugs that have been adequate in terms of dosage and duration (Barnes, 2011). With regard to delusional beliefs in particular, the duration of illness (untreated) is related to the effectiveness of pharmacological, and likely psychological, interventions: With many years to entrench belief systems, time to spend gathering evidence and the potential progressive brain changes seen in the early years of psychosis, less response to therapies may occur. Drake and colleagues clearly showed some time ago that the length of untreated psychosis corresponded to the severity of positive symptoms at first presentation and the response to treatment (Drake, Haley, Akhtar, & Lewis, 2000).

Similarly to BAP guidance, the National Institute for Health and Care Excellence (NICE) recommendations for the treatment of schizophrenia and psychosis include the prescription of an antipsychotic medication (in combination with psychological interventions) as the first step in the treatment of psychosis (Kuipers, Yesufu-Udechuku, Taylor, & Kendall, 2014):

> The choice of antipsychotic medication should be made by the service user and healthcare professional together, taking into account the views of the carer if the service user agrees. Provide information and discuss the likely benefits and possible side effects of each drug, including: metabolic (including weight gain and diabetes) extrapyramidal (including akathisia, dyskinesia and dystonia) cardiovascular (including prolonging the QT interval) hormonal (including increasing plasma prolactin) other (including unpleasant subjective experiences).

NICE guidelines are not without controversy, as highlighted by open debate in the British Journal of Psychiatry (Kendall et al., 2016). NICE gives equal or indeed enhanced emphasis on psychological over pharmacological interventions, including cognitive behavioural therapy for psychosis (CBTp) and art therapy, which have a considerably less developed evidence base and thus the guideline has been said to have shown a negative bias to drug treatment. The Scottish Intercollegiate Guideline Network (SIGN) is the Scottish equivalent to NICE. Whist both guidelines have a number of similarities, for example recommending the use of antipsychotics (including clozapine when needed), family intervention, early interventions, assertive community treatment and CBTp, SIGN offer more extensive recommendation on pharmacological treatment, with some 60% of its recommendations devoted to pharmacological interventions alone(Taylor & Perera, 2015). The argument of bias of NICE towards psychosocial interventions was felt to be based on a belief that antipsychotic medications are more potentially harmful. There is an absence of evidence for adverse effects of psychosocial interventions; however the argument is that the absence of evidence is not the same as evidence of absence.

In terms of medication choice, as BAP guidance's state, this should be based on individual patient presentation and choice, as there is no clear evidence to suggest one antipsychotic medication is likely to be more effective than another within an individual patient trial with the exception of clozapine. The European First Episode Schizophrenia Trial (EUFEST) tested haloperidol against several 'second generation antipsychotic medications' in first-episode schizophrenia and schizophreniform disorder. All medications showed an effect on positive symptoms with a mean symptomatic improvement of more than 60% (Kahn et al., 2008), thus choice should be made on the balance of side effects, previous history of response and with patient choice.

S.A. writes:

> It's very important for clinicians to offer people a choice in the medication they are prescribed, and to be prepared to switch medications if the side effects can't be tolerated. Personally I felt embarrassed about some of my side effects so I think it's important clinicians ask about them directly.

In addition, epidemiological evidence is clear on the effectiveness, and safety, of antipsychotic medication. In a cohort of over 20,000 people in a Swedish database study demonstrated the effectiveness of antipsychotic medication in terms or treatment, prevention of relapse and hospitalization. Clozapine and long acting injections were superior to other forms of medication, likely the result of increase efficacy (clozapine) and concordance monitoring (both) (Tiihonen et al., 2017).

Lally et al. have also recently demonstrated optimistic remission and recovery figures in treated first episode psychosis, with remission in nearly 60% of people at 5 years remaining well (Lally, J. et al. 2017). Antipsychotic medication is effective in the prevention of relapse and randomized controlled trials strongly support the efficacy of antipsychotics for the acute treatment of psychosis and prevention of relapse (Goff et al., 2017; Leucht et al., 2012) There is also growing opinion that a significant minority of people can remain well on very low dose medication after the treatment of the acute episode (Murray et al., 2016). In contrast, meta-analysis conducted by Vermeulen showed an increased long-term mortality risk in patients with schizophrenia who did not use antipsychotic medication during follow up (Vermeulen et al., 2017). Thus in clinical decision, individual formulation including risks of relapse is needed, with careful consideration of positive effects and side-effects of medication including propensity to cause sedation and weight gain or stiffness, rigidity and tremor, balanced by the prevention of return of delusions and hallucinations, and reduced risk of suicidal behaviour (Barnes, 2011). A focus on the treatment of delusions beliefs themselves should not detract from effective treatments of the impact delusional beliefs may bring. We have recently demonstrated the effectiveness of antidepressants in the treatment of depression in schizophrenia (Gregory, Mallikarjun, & Upthegrove, 2017) and Helfer has also demonstrated the long term role of antidepressants in suicide prevention in psychotic disorders and their safe use in combination with antipsychotic medication (Helfer et al., 2016).

Psychological Therapy

Cognitive therapy is a predominent psychological treatment is used in the majority of mental health disorders with differing levels of proven efficacy. Fairly robust evidence exists for Cognitive Behavioural Therapy (CBT) in depression and anxiety (Clark, 2011). Historically, the concept of psychological therapy for delusional beliefs was not encouraged: concern that targeting delusions directly was likely to make matters worse, within an understanding that delusions were not amenable to reason nor subject to 'normal' mechanisms of learning, and therefore talking through the evidence was counterproductive. In fact this position was unrelated to Jaspers first accounts of delusional beliefs and logical reasoning, which did not equate to a therapeutic nihilism, yet did lead to a lack of focus of psychological therapies for psychosis for some decades.

However Cognitive Behaviour Therapy for psychosis (CBTp) now has an evidence base, although the strength of this base is debated. The effectiveness of CBTp has been assessed by measuring change in positive symptoms (hallucinations and delusions), negative symptoms, quality of life and functioning such that CBTp is now recommended by National Guidelines as rehearsed above (Kuipers et al., 2014). The effectiveness of psychological therapies are not uncontroversial as studies mostly compare CBTp to treatment as usual (Kendall et al., 2016). When compared to an active comparison group, such as befriending, CBTp has less clear evidence. Turkington et al. demonstrate befriending to be particularly useful for persecutory delusions (Turkington 2017). CBTp generally aims to reduce positive symptoms, negative symptoms and improves general functioning (Wykes, Steel, Everitt, & Tarrier, 2008) and national guidelines currently recommend CBTp for patients with schizophrenia in all phases of the disorder (Kuipers et al., 2014).

With respect to delusional beliefs, only a small number of studies have reported efficacy on delusional beliefs specifically in CBTp trials, or investigated delusional beliefs as the primary outcome, with meta-analysis showing a smaller effect size on delusions compared to hallucinations (van der Gaag, Valmaggia, & Smit, 2014). Given the prevalence of persecutory as opposed to other delusions, those studies designed to assess the effect of CBTp on delusions mainly focus here. Freeman and et al. examined the effect of CBTp on thirty participants in a single blind RCT and found a significant reduction in paranoia, but also significant improvements in well-being, self-esteem and depression (Freeman et al., 2014). As rehearsed above, given the significance of depression and suicidal thinking in response to delusions and in the generation of positive symptoms, this is not unimportant.

Although the evidence base for CBTp may be less than perfect, the historical assumption that CBT should not be used in psychosis has been dispelled. In practice, the objectives of psychological therapy are agreed by the patient and therapist in collaboration, and in psychosis may include distressing beliefs, or depression or an entirely different focus. Changing a belief, 'getting rid' of the delusions may well not be the focus of therapy, rather this may include stopping or reducing the time spent thinking about (or acting upon) a belief. However, when focused on delusional beliefs, Turkington proposes that during the cognitive therapy process, expectation is that even primary delusions might become more understandable as the patient's life history and belief profile are made apparent. Techniques involved may include peripheral questioning and inference chaining to explore beliefs once a therapeutic alliance is formed (Turkington & Siddle, 1998). For example, with Andrew one might discuss an inference question chain such as:

Andrew: "MI5 are training me."
Therapist: "What does it mean for you to believe this?"
Andrew: "There is a reason for everything I've been through."
Therapist: "What does this mean to you to understand this?"
Andrew: "I will be rewarded, money, in the end, for what's been done to me. I don't want to have to do the work, I'd rather have a quiet life, but if I have to this, then maybe at least they will reward me".

There is growing debate about the size of difference can be expected from CBTp; Jauhar found only small differences between CBTp and control groups, which were not significant when only studies that had an active control were pooled (Jauhar et al., 2014). Publication bias and unblinded studies are also highlighted. A more recent meta-analysis of 19 RCT's comparing CBTp and reporting delusions as an outcome found a significant effect with a small to medium effect size that was maintained at 42 weeks when compared to treatment as usual. However in sub-analysis of 8 studies that compared CBTp to another active psychological intervention, there were no significant differences at end of therapy or later follow up (Mehl, Werner, & Lincoln, 2015). In later studies CBTp was compared to a wide range of interventions supportive counselling (Durham et al., 2003; Lewis et al., 2002; Valmaggia, Van Der Gaag, Tarrier, Pijnenborg, & Slooff, 2005), attention placebo (O'Connor et al., 2007), psychoeducation (Cather et al., 2005) problem solving (Philippa A

Garety et al., 2008; Tarrier et al., 2014) and social activity therapy (Haddock, Lowens, Brosnan, Barrowclough, & Novaco, 2004).

NICE currently recommends CBTp, highlighting the importance of offering this in conjunction with antipsychotic medication, or on its own if medication is declined, as part of a broad-based approach that combines different treatment options tailored to the needs of individual service users (Kuipers et al., 2014). In summary, however it appears psychological therapy may have a beneficial effect in delusional beliefs, and this may be in acting mainly on 'peripheral' but clinically useful targets of distress, depression and acting on beliefs rather than changing the core beliefs system itself.

1.8 Conclusion

Psychiatrists are concerned with delusional beliefs because, as all physicians should be, they are interested in human experience and driven by a need to offer therapeutic options to people in need. In general, we become physicians through a combined desire to understand the human condition and to help, be this though biological or other vehicles. The rich descriptions of patient experience in individuals with delusional beliefs are unparalleled in other branches of medicine. Delusional beliefs are at the heart of psychiatry, capturing the essence of this drive to understand and offer real therapeutic opportunity, alleviate suffering, and improve lives. At its best this involves a shared understanding of the context of beliefs, personal meaning and impact. Increasingly we also understand more about the potential biological pathways to delusional thinking, and effectiveness of both pharmacological and psychological interventions. However, the primacy remains of understanding the context in which delusional beliefs are experienced in the round; the role of delusional mood, depression, mania, hallucinations and other positive symptoms, trauma and distress. This has long been recognised to be at the heart of developing a therapeutic relationship, and only when this is established can treatment options be discussed.

References

APA. (2013). *DSM 5*. American Psychiatric Association.

Arnone, D., McKie, S., Elliott, R., Juhasz, G., Thomas, E., Downey, D., … Anderson, I. (2013). State-dependent changes in hippocampal grey matter in depression. *Molecular Psychiatry, 18*(12), 1265–1272.

Barnes, T. R., & S. C. G. o. t. B. A. f. P. (2011). Evidence-based guidelines for the pharmacological treatment of schizophrenia: Recommendations from the British Association for Psychopharmacology. *Journal of Psychopharmacology, 25*(5), 567–620. https://doi.org/10.1177/0269881110391123

Bebbington, P., & Freeman, D. (2017). Transdiagnostic extension of delusions: Schizophrenia and beyond. *Schizophrenia Bulletin, 43*(2), 273–282.

Birchwood, M., Gilbert, P., Gilbert, J., Trower, P., Meaden, A., Hay, J., … Miles, J. N. (2004). Interpersonal and role-related schema influence the relationship with the dominant 'voice'in schizophrenia: A comparison of three models. *Psychological Medicine, 34*(8), 1571–1580.

Broome, M. R. (2013). *The Maudsley reader in phenomenological psychiatry*. Cambridge, UK: Cambridge University Press.

Broome, M. R., He, Z., Iftikhar, M., Eyden, J., & Marwaha, S. (2015). Neurobiological and behavioural studies of affective instability in clinical populations: A systematic review. *Neuroscience & Biobehavioral Reviews, 51*, 243–254.

Broome, M. R., Johns, L., Valli, I., Woolley, J., Tabraham, P., Brett, C., … McGuire, P. (2007). Delusion formation and reasoning biases in those at clinical high risk for psychosis. *The British Journal of Psychiatry, 191*(51), s38–s42.

Brunet, K., Birchwood, M., Upthegrove, R., Michail, M., & Ross, K. (2012). A prospective study of PTSD following recovery from first-episode psychosis: The threat from persecutors, voices, and patienthood. *British Journal of Clinical Psychology, 51*(4), 418–433.

Busatto, G. F. (2013). Structural and functional neuroimaging studies in major depressive disorder with psychotic features: A critical review. *Schizophrenia Bulletin, 39*(4), 776–786.

Cannon, M., Clarke, M. C., & Cotter, D. R. (2014). Priming the brain for psychosis: Maternal inflammation during fetal development and the risk of later psychiatric disorder. *American Journal of Psychiatry, 171*, 91–94.

Cather, C., Penn, D., Otto, M. W., Yovel, I., Mueser, K. T., & Goff, D. C. (2005). A pilot study of functional Cognitive Behavioral Therapy (fCBT) for schizophrenia. *Schizophrenia Research, 74*(2), 201–209.

Catone, G., Marwaha, S., Kuipers, E., Lennox, B., Freeman, D., Bebbington, P., & Broome, M. (2015). Bullying victimisation and risk of psychotic phenomena: Analyses of British national survey data. *The Lancet Psychiatry, 2*(7), 618–624.

Chisholm, B., Freeman, D., & Cooke, A. (2006). Identifying potential predictors of traumatic reactions to psychotic episodes. *British Journal of Clinical Psychology, 45*(4), 545–559.

Clark, D. M. (2011). Implementing NICE guidelines for the psychological treatment of depression and anxiety disorders: The IAPT experience. *International Review of Psychiatry, 23*(4), 318–327.

Cornblatt, B. A., Lencz, T., Smith, C. W., Correll, C. U., Auther, A. M., & Nakayama, E. (2003). The schizophrenia prodrome revisited: A neurodevelopmental perspective. *Schizophrenia Bulletin, 29*(4), 633–651.

Daalman, K., Diederen, K., Derks, E. M., van Lutterveld, R., Kahn, R. S., & Sommer, I. E. (2012). Childhood trauma and auditory verbal hallucinations. *Psychological Medicine, 42*(12), 2475–2484.

Drake, R. J., Haley, C. J., Akhtar, S., & Lewis, S. W. (2000). Causes and consequences of duration of untreated psychosis in schizophrenia. *The British Journal of Psychiatry, 177*(6), 511–515.

Durham, R. C., Guthrie, M., Morton, R. V., Reid, D. A., Treliving, L. R., Fowler, D., & MacDonald, R. R. (2003). Tayside—Fife clinical trial of cognitive—Behavioural therapy for medication-resistant psychotic symptoms. *The British Journal of Psychiatry, 182*(4), 303–311.

Etain, B., Henry, C., Bellivier, F., Mathieu, F., & Leboyer, M. (2008). Beyond genetics: Childhood affective trauma in bipolar disorder. *Bipolar Disorders, 10*(8), 867–876.

Fenton, W. S., McGlashan, T. H., Victor, B. J., & Blyler, C. R. (1997). Symptoms, subtype, and suicidality in patients with schizophrenia spectrum disorders. *The American Journal of Psychiatry, 154*(2), 199–204.

Freeman, D., Garety, P. A., & Kuipers, E. (2001). Persecutory delusions: Developing the understanding of belief maintenance and emotional distress. *Psychological Medicine, 31*(7), 1293–1306.

Freeman, D., Garety, P. A., Kuipers, E., Fowler, D., Bebbington, P. E., & Dunn, G. (2007). Acting on persecutory delusions: The importance of safety seeking. *Behaviour Research and Therapy, 45*(1), 89–99.

Freeman, D., Pugh, K., Dunn, G., Evans, N., Sheaves, B., Waite, F., … Fowler, D. (2014). An early Phase II randomised controlled trial testing the effect on persecutory delusions of using CBT to reduce negative cognitions about the self: The potential benefits of enhancing self confidence. *Schizophrenia Research, 160*(1), 186–192.

Garety, P. A., Fowler, D. G., Freeman, D., Bebbington, P., Dunn, G., & Kuipers, E. (2008). Cognitive–behavioural therapy and family intervention for relapse prevention and symptom reduction in psychosis: Randomised controlled trial. *The British Journal of Psychiatry, 192*(6), 412–423.

Garety, P. A., & Freeman, D. (1999). Cognitive approaches to delusions: A critical review of theories and evidence. *The British Journal of Clinical Psychology / The British Psychological Society, 38.*(Pt 2, 113–154.

Garety, P. A., Kuipers, E., Fowler, D., Freeman, D., & Bebbington, P. (2001). A cognitive model of the positive symptoms of psychosis. *Psychological Medicine, 31*(2), 189–195.

Gilbert, P., Birchwood, M., Gilbert, J., Trower, P., Hay, J., Murray, B., … Miles, J. N. (2001). An exploration of evolved mental mechanisms for dominant and subordinate behaviour in relation to auditory hallucinations in schizophrenia and critical thoughts in depression. *Psychological Medicine, 31*(6), 1117–1127.

Goff, D. C., Falkai, P., Fleischhacker, W. W., Girgis, R. R., Kahn, R. M., Uchida, H., ... Lieberman, J. A. (2017). The long-term effects of antipsychotic medication on clinical course in schizophrenia. *American Journal of Psychiatry, 174*(9), 840–849.

Gregory, A., Mallikarjun, P., & Upthegrove, R. (2017). Treatment of depression in schizophrenia: Systematic review and meta-analysis. *The British Journal of Psychiatry, 211*, 198–204.

Haddock, G., Lowens, I., Brosnan, N., Barrowclough, C., & Novaco, R. W. (2004). Cognitive-behaviour therapy for inpatients with psychosis and anger problems within a low secure environment. *Behavioural and Cognitive Psychotherapy, 32*(1), 77–98.

Helfer, B., Samara, M. T., Huhn, M., Klupp, E., Leucht, C., Zhu, Y., ... Leucht, S. (2016). Efficacy and safety of antidepressants added to antipsychotics for schizophrenia: A systematic review and meta-analysis. *American Journal of Psychiatry, 173*, 876.

Howes, O. D., Kambeitz, J., Kim, E., Stahl, D., Slifstein, M., Abi-Dargham, A., & Kapur, S. (2012). The nature of dopamine dysfunction in schizophrenia and what this means for treatment: Meta-analysis of imaging studies. *Archives of General Psychiatry, 69*(8), 776–786.

Huber, G., & Gross, G. (1989). The concept of basic symptoms in schizophrenic and schizoaffective psychoses. *Recenti Progressi in Medicina, 80*(12), 646–652.

Jaspers, K. (1997). *General psychopathology* (Vol. 2). Baltimore, MD: JHU Press.

Jauhar, S., McKenna, P., Radua, J., Fung, E., Salvador, R., & Laws, K. (2014). Cognitive-behavioural therapy for the symptoms of schizophrenia: Systematic review and meta-analysis with examination of potential bias. *The British Journal of Psychiatry, 204*(1), 20–29.

Kahn, R. S., Fleischhacker, W. W., Boter, H., Davidson, M., Vergouwe, Y., Keet, I. P., ... Libiger, J. (2008). Effectiveness of antipsychotic drugs in first-episode schizophrenia and schizophreniform disorder: An open randomised clinical trial. *The Lancet, 371*(9618), 1085–1097.

Kapur, S. (2003). Psychosis as a state of aberrant salience: A framework linking biology, phenomenology, and pharmacology in schizophrenia. *American Journal of Psychiatry, 160*(1), 13–23.

Kelleher, I., & Cannon, M. (2011). Psychotic-like experiences in the general population: Characterizing a high-risk group for psychosis. *Psychological Medicine, 41*, 1), 1–1), 6.

Kendall, T., Whittington, C. J., Kuipers, E., Johnson, S., Birchwood, M. J., Marshall, M., & Morrison, A. P. (2016). NICE v. SIGN on psychosis and schizophrenia: Same roots, similar guidelines, different interpretations. *The British Journal of Psychiatry, 208*(4), 316–319.

Kesting, M.-L., & Lincoln, T. M. (2013). The relevance of self-esteem and self-schemas to persecutory delusions: A systematic review. *Comprehensive Psychiatry, 54*(7), 766–789.

Kuipers, E., Yesufu-Udechuku, A., Taylor, C., & Kendall, T. (2014). Management of psychosis and schizophrenia in adults: Summary of updated NICE guidance. *BMJ: British Medical Journal, 348*, g1173.

Kumari, V., Peters, E., Guinn, A., Fannon, D., Russell, T., Sumich, A., … Williams, S. C. (2015). Mapping depression in schizophrenia: A functional magnetic resonance imaging study. *Schizophrenia Bulletin, 42*, 802–813.

Lally, J., Ajnakina, O., Stubbs, B., Cullinane, M., Murphy, K. C., Gaughran, F., & Murray, R. M. (2017). Remission and recovery from first-episode psychosis in adults: Systematic review and meta-analysis of long-term outcome studies. *The British Journal of Psychiatry: the Journal of Mental Science, 211*(6), 350–358.

Lataster, T., Valmaggia, L., Lardinois, M., van Os, J., & Myin-Germeys, I. (2013). Increased stress reactivity: A mechanism specifically associated with the positive symptoms of psychotic disorder. *Psychological Medicine, 43*(7), 1389–1400. https://doi.org/10.1017/S0033291712002279

Lee, S.-H., Niznikiewicz, M., Asami, T., Otsuka, T., Salisbury, D. F., Shenton, M. E., & McCarley, R. W. (2015). Initial and progressive gray matter abnormalities in insular gyrus and temporal pole in first-episode schizophrenia contrasted with first-episode affective psychosis. *Schizophrenia Bulletin*. https://doi.org/10.1093/schbul/sbv177

Leucht, S., Tardy, M., Komossa, K., Heres, S., Kissling, W., Salanti, G., & Davis, J. M. (2012). Antipsychotic drugs versus placebo for relapse prevention in schizophrenia: A systematic review and meta-analysis. *The Lancet, 379*(9831), 2063–2071.

Lewis, S., Tarrier, N., Haddock, G., Bentall, R., Kinderman, P., Kingdon, D., … Leadley, K. (2002). Randomised controlled trial of cognitive—Behavioural therapy in early schizophrenia: Acute-phase outcomes. *The British Journal of Psychiatry, 181*(43), s91–s97.

Maj, M. (2013). *Karl jaspers and the genesis of delusions in schizophrenia*. Oxford: Oxford University Press US.

Marwaha, S., Thompson, A., Upthegrove, R., & Broome, M. R. (2016). 15 Years on—Early Intervention for a new generation. *Bristish Journal of Psychiatry, 209*(3), 186–188.

Mehl, S., Werner, D., & Lincoln, T. M. (2015). Does Cognitive Behavior Therapy for psychosis show a sustainable effect on delusions? A meta-analysis. *Frontiers in Psychology, 6*, 1450.

Michail, M., & Birchwood, M. (2009). Social anxiety disorder in first-episode psychosis: Incidence, phenomenology and relationship with paranoia. *The British Journal of Psychiatry, 195*(3), 234–241.

Mishara, A. L., & Fusar-Poli, P. (2013). The phenomenology and neurobiology of delusion formation during psychosis onset: Jaspers, Truman symptoms, and aberrant salience. *Schizophrenia Bulletin, 39*(2), 278–286.
Mondelli, V., Cattaneo, A., Murri, M. B., Di Forti, M., Handley, R., Hepgul, N., … Aitchison, K. J. (2011). Stress and inflammation reduce brain-derived neurotrophic factor expression in first-episode psychosis: A pathway to smaller hippocampal volume. *The Journal of Clinical Psychiatry, 72*(12), 1478–1684.
Murray, G., Corlett, P., Clark, L., Pessiglione, M., Blackwell, A., Honey, G., … Fletcher, P. (2008). How dopamine dysregulation leads to psychotic symptoms? Abnormal mesolimbic and mesostriatal prediction error signalling in psychosis. *Molecular Psychiatry, 13*(3), 239.
Murray, R. M., Quattrone, D., Natesan, S., van Os, J., Nordentoft, M., Howes, O., … Taylor, D. (2016). Should psychiatrists be more cautious about the long-term prophylactic use of antipsychotics? *The British Journal of Psychiatry, 209*(5), 361–365.
Nelson, B., Yuen, H. P., Wood, S. J., Lin, A., Spiliotacopoulos, D., Bruxner, A., … Yung, A. R. (2013). Long-term follow-up of a group at ultra high risk ("prodromal") for psychosis: The PACE 400 study. *JAMA Psychiatry, 70*(8), 793–802. https://doi.org/10.1001/jamapsychiatry.2013.1270
Neria, Y., Nandi, A., & Galea, S. (2008). Post-traumatic stress disorder following disasters: A systematic review. *Psychological Medicine, 38*(4), 467–480.
Noto, C., Ota, V. K., Santoro, M. L., Ortiz, B. B., Rizzo, L. B., Higuchi, C. H., … Gadelha, A. (2015). Effects of depression on the cytokine profile in drug naive first-episode psychosis. *Schizophrenia Research, 164*(1), 53–58.
O'Connor, K., Stip, E., Pélissier, M.-C., Aardema, F., Guay, S., Gaudette, G., … Careau, Y. (2007). Treating delusional disorder: A comparison of cognitive-behavioural therapy and attention placebo control. *The Canadian Journal of Psychiatry, 52*(3), 182–190.
Oyebode, F. (2014). *Sims' symptoms in the mind: Textbook of descriptive psychopathology*. Philadelphia: Elsevier Health Sciences.
Palaniyappan, L., Mallikarjun, P., Joseph, V., White, T., & Liddle, P. (2011). Reality distortion is related to the structure of the salience network in schizophrenia. *Psychological Medicine, 41*(8), 1701–1708.
Perälä, J., Suvisaari, J., Saarni, S. I., Kuoppasalmi, K., Isometsä, E., Pirkola, S., … Kieseppä, T. (2007). Lifetime prevalence of psychotic and bipolar I disorders in a general population. *Archives of General Psychiatry, 64*(1), 19–28.
Pierre, J. M. (2010). Hallucinations in nonpsychotic disorders: Toward a differential diagnosis of "hearing voices". *Harvard Review of Psychiatry, 18*(1), 22–35.
Reniers, R. L., Lin, A., Yung, A. R., Koutsouleris, N., Nelson, B., Cropley, V. L., … Wood, S. J. (2017). Neuroanatomical predictors of functional outcome in individuals at ultra-high risk for psychosis. *Schizophrenia Bulletin, 43*(2), 449–458.

Rüsch, N., Angermeyer, M. C., & Corrigan, P. W. (2005). Mental illness stigma: Concepts, consequences, and initiatives to reduce stigma. *European Psychiatry, 20*(8), 529–539. https://doi.org/10.1016/j.eurpsy.2005.04.004

Sandhu, A., Ives, J., Birchwood, M., & Upthegrove, R. (2013). The subjective experience and phenomenology of depression following first episode psychosis: A qualitative study using photo-elicitation. *Journal of Affective Disorders, 149*(1), 166–174.

Schultze-Lutter, F., Klosterkötter, J., & Ruhrmann, S. (2014). Improving the clinical prediction of psychosis by combining ultra-high risk criteria and cognitive basic symptoms. *Schizophrenia Research, 154*(1), 100–106.

Schultze-Lutter, F., Ruhrmann, S., Berning, J., Maier, W., & Klosterkötter, J. (2008). Basic symptoms and ultrahigh risk criteria: Symptom development in the initial prodromal state. *Schizophrenia Bulletin, 36*(1), 182–191.

Smieskova, R., Fusar-Poli, P., Allen, P., Bendfeldt, K., Stieglitz, R., Drewe, J., … Borgwardt, S. (2010). Neuroimaging predictors of transition to psychosis—A systematic review and meta-analysis. *Neuroscience & Biobehavioral Reviews, 34*(8), 1207–1222.

Stanghellini, G., & Fuchs, T. (2013). *One century of Karl Jaspers' general psychopathology*. Oxford: Oxford University Press.

Staring, A., Van der Gaag, M., Van den Berge, M., Duivenvoorden, H., & Mulder, C. (2009). Stigma moderates the associations of insight with depressed mood, low self-esteem, and low quality of life in patients with schizophrenia spectrum disorders. *Schizophrenia Research, 115*(2), 363–369.

Tarrier, N., Kelly, J., Maqsood, S., Snelson, N., Maxwell, J., Law, H., … Gooding, P. (2014). The cognitive behavioural prevention of suicide in psychosis: A clinical trial. *Schizophrenia Research, 156*(2), 204–210.

Taylor, M., & Perera, U. (2015). NICE CG178 Psychosis and Schizophrenia in Adults: Treatment and Management–an evidence-based guideline? *RCP*.

Tiihonen, J., Mittendorfer-Rutz, E., Majak, M., Mehtälä, J., Hoti, F., Jedenius, E., … Tanskanen, A. (2017). Real-world effectiveness of antipsychotic treatments in a nationwide cohort of 29 823 patients with schizophrenia. *JAMA Psychiatry, 74*(7), 686–693.

Turkington, D., & Siddle, R. (1998). Cognitive therapy for the treatment of delusions. *Advances in Psychiatric Treatment, 4*(4), 235–241.

Upthegrove, R., Birchwood, M., Ross, K., Brunett, K., McCollum, R., & Jones, L. (2010). The evolution of depression and suicidality in first episode psychosis. *Acta Psychiatrica Scandinavica, 122*(3), 211–218. https://doi.org/10.1111/j.1600-0447.2009.01506.x

Upthegrove, R., Broome, M., Caldwell, K., Ives, J., Oyebode, F., & Wood, S. (2015). Understanding auditory verbal hallucinations: A systematic review of current evidence. *Acta Psychiatrica Scandinavica, 133*, 352–367.

Upthegrove, R., Chard, C., Jones, L., Gordon-Smith, K., Forty, L., Jones, I., & Craddock, N. (2015). Adverse childhood events and psychosis in bipolar affective disorder. *The British Journal of Psychiatry, 206*(3), 191–197.

Upthegrove, R., Ives, J., Broome, M. R., Caldwell, K., Wood, S. J., & Oyebode, F. (2016). Auditory verbal hallucinations in first-episode psychosis: A phenomenological investigation. *British Journal of Psychiatry Open, 2*(1), 88–95.

Upthegrove, R., Manzanares-Teson, N., & Barnes, N. M. (2014). Cytokine function in medication-naive first episode psychosis: A systematic review and meta-analysis. *Schizophrenia Research, 155*(1), 101–108.

Upthegrove, R., Marwaha, S., & Birchwood, M. (2016). Depression and schizophrenia: Cause, consequence or trans-diagnostic issue? *Schizophrenia Bulletin*, sbw097.

Upthegrove, R., Ross, K., Brunet, K., McCollum, R., & Jones, L. (2014). Depression in first episode psychosis: The role of subordination and shame. *Psychiatry Research, 217*(3), 177–184.

Valmaggia, L. R., Van Der Gaag, M., Tarrier, N., Pijnenborg, M., & Slooff, C. J. (2005). Cognitive–behavioural therapy for refractory psychotic symptoms of schizophrenia resistant to atypical antipsychotic medication. *The British Journal of Psychiatry, 186*(4), 324–330.

van der Gaag, M., Valmaggia, L. R., & Smit, F. (2014). The effects of individually tailored formulation-based cognitive behavioural therapy in auditory hallucinations and delusions: A meta-analysis. *Schizophrenia Research, 156*(1), 30–37.

Vermeulen, J., van Rooijen, G., Doedens, P., Numminen, E., van Tricht, M., & de Haan, L. (2017). Antipsychotic medication and long-term mortality risk in patients with schizophrenia; a systematic review and meta-analysis. *Psychological Medicine, 47*(13), 2217–2228.

Wykes, T., Steel, C., Everitt, B., & Tarrier, N. (2008). Cognitive behavior therapy for schizophrenia: Effect sizes, clinical models, and methodological rigor. *Schizophrenia Bulletin, 34*(3), 523–537.

Yung, A. R., Nelson, B., Stanford, C., Simmons, M. B., Cosgrave, E. M., Killackey, E., … McGorry, P. D. (2008). Validation of "prodromal" criteria to detect individuals at ultra high risk of psychosis: 2 year follow-up. *Schizophrenia Research, 105*(1–3), 10–17.

Yung, A. R., Pan Yuen, H., Mcgorry, P. D., Phillips, L. J., Kelly, D., Dell'olio, M., … Buckby, J. (2005). Mapping the onset of psychosis: The comprehensive assessment of at-risk mental states. *Australian and New Zealand Journal of Psychiatry, 39*(11–12), 964–971. https://doi.org/10.1080/j.1440-1614.2005.01714.x

BY

CHAPTER 2

Delusions and Prediction Error

Philip Corlett

Abstract Different empirical and theoretical traditions approach delusions differently. This chapter is about how cognitive neuroscience – the practice of studying the brain to draw conclusions about the mind – has been applied to the problem of belief and delusion. In particular, the focus is on a particular bridging theory, that of predictive coding. This theory holds that the brain contains a model of the world (and the self as an agent in that world). It uses that model to make predictions in order to adapt to the environment. Errors in those predictions can garner belief updating or be ignored, depending on how each prediction error response sustains adaptive fitness. The discussion will cover how delusions might arise and be maintained under the influence of aberrant prediction errors and what psychological and neural mechanisms of prediction error processing pertain to delusions, comparing and contrasting the theory with other prominent theories of delusions. The conclusion is that the single factor, prediction error account gives a parsimonious account of delusions that generates novel predictions about how best to treat delusions and incorporates numerous biological, clinical and phenomenological data regarding delusions.

P. Corlett (✉)
Connecticut Mental Health Center, New Haven, CT, USA
e-mail: philip.corlett@yale.edu

L. Bortolotti (ed.), *Delusions in Context*,
https://doi.org/10.1007/978-3-319-97202-2_2

Keywords Aberrant prediction errors • Belief updating • Cognitive neuroscience • Delusions • Predictive coding • Prediction error processing

2.1 A Millennial Cult and the Psychology of Delusion

Defining, explaining and ultimately understanding delusions has proven challenging. There are many instances of people adopting and acting upon beliefs that appear delusional, despite an apparent lack of serious mental illness.

One real-world historical example may be particularly instructive.

The Chicago Tribune reported, in December 1954, that Dr. Charles Laughead (a Christian with a fascination with UFOs) foresaw the end of the world. He was speaking on behalf of Dorothy Martin, who was supposedly relaying a prophecy from extra-terrestrials from the planet Clarion. The prophecy of course did not manifest. Martin was placed in psychiatric care and charged with contributing to the delinquency of minors – the children that she and Laughead warned of the forthcoming apocalypse were so scared they had trouble sleeping.

Martin ultimately settled in Sedona, Arizona where she lived until she was 92, continuing to proselytize about aliens, but ultimately evading interaction with psychiatric services. Did Martin have delusions? What about her acolytes? Their beliefs were certainly bizarre and firm and occasionally held with some distress. There is growing appreciation that strong beliefs and delusions exist on a continuum and may be difficult to distinguish (DSM-V). This is a challenge. However, there are also opportunities. The psychology and neurobiology of belief may inform our understanding and treatment of delusions – which is a clear unmet clinical need.

Unbeknownst to Martin and Laughead, some of their followers were social psychologists from the University of Minnesota, led by Leon Festinger. The academics studied the group as the end-times loomed, resulting in a book; *'When Prophecy Fails: A social psychological study of a modern group that predicted the destruction of the world'* (Festinger, Riecken, & Schachter, 1956). The authors focused on cognitive dissonance; the internal discord felt from holding conflicting beliefs simultaneously [in this case was between the prophecy and real-world events (Festinger,

1962)]. People in the cult acted to reduce their dissonance. Many disavowed the apocalypse and left the group. However, some *increased* their conviction in the face of contradictory data. Martin's failed predictions were re-contextualized as actually having come to fruition (a minor earthquake did occur in California). Confounded expectations were explained away ("the aliens did come for us, but they were scared off by the crowds of press"). These sleights of mind (McKay, Langdon, & Coltheart, 2005) will be familiar to those who have spoken to patients with delusions (Garety, 1991, 1992), who can respond to challenges to their beliefs by incorporating the challenging data, and sometimes the challenger, into their delusional narrative.

Cognitive dissonance contains the kernel of the prediction error account of delusions. In brief, when beliefs abut reality, prediction errors result – which are mismatches between expectation and experience. One may update one's beliefs or ignore conflicting data – minimizing the conflict. When conflict is detected inappropriately, delusions result (Adams, Stephan, Brown, Frith, & Friston, 2013; Corlett, 2015; Corlett & Fletcher, 2014; Corlett, Frith, & Fletcher, 2009a; Corlett, Honey, & Fletcher, 2007; Corlett, Honey, Krystal, & Fletcher, 2010; Corlett, Taylor, Wang, Fletcher, & Krystal, 2010; Fletcher & Frith, 2009; Gray, Feldon, Rawlins, Hemsley, & Smith, 1991)

2.2 Reasoning About Beliefs from Biology, Psychology, and Cognitive Neuroscience

Delusions are challenging to study in the laboratory – the sufferer often denies any problem (Gibbs & David, 2003) and does not present to clinical attention until delusions are fully formed (Corlett et al., 2007). The neural correlates of hallucinations can be captured when people experiencing them report their experiences in a functional imaging scanner (Zmigrod, Garrison, Carr, & Simons, 2016). Delusions on the other hand, do not typically wax and wane on a timescale that lends itself to such capture. Experimental models can provide a unique window onto an otherwise inaccessible disease process (Corlett et al., 2007). Prior work has capitalized on one such drug model of delusions: ketamine; the NMDA glutamate receptor antagonist drug that transiently and reversibly engenders delusion-like ideas in healthy people (Pomarol-Clotet et al., 2006) and other animals (Honsberger, Taylor, & Corlett, 2015).

These delusions might be manifestations of aberrant prediction errors (Corlett, Taylor, et al., 2010), the mismatch between what we expect and what we experience (Rescorla & Wagner, 1972). Derived from formal learning theory to explain mechanisms of animal conditioning, prediction error (Rescorla & Wagner, 1972) is signaled by dopamine and glutamate activity in the brain (Lavin et al., 2005). It has also become a key process in theoretical models of human causal learning and belief formation (Dickinson, 2001). By minimizing prediction error we model the causal structure of our environment (Dickinson, 2001). If prediction errors occur when they ought not to, aberrant associations are formed and strengthened, culminating in delusional beliefs.

Beliefs and the Brain

The cognitive neuroscience of belief has been slow to develop. The absence of a consilient psychological theory of belief formation led the late Jerry Fodor – both a philosopher and a cognitive scientist, to assert that, whilst beliefs are among the most interesting cognitive phenomena, they are not ready to be explained in the same cognitive and neural terms as more accessible processes, such as vision (Fodor, 1975, 2000). However, there are now cognitive and neural frameworks of belief (Dickinson, 2001) amenable to quantitative analysis and applicable to studies on healthy subjects (Corlett et al., 2004) in clinical settings (Corlett, Frith, & Fletcher, 2009b; Corlett, Taylor, et al., 2010), and across species (Dickinson, 2001).

A Bridging Hypothesis: From Mind to Brain?

Associationists believe that the mind is a network of associations between ideas (Warren, 1921). It began with Plato (Plato, 350 B.C./1999). Aristotle outlined the first laws of association (Aristotle, 350 B.C./1930). John Locke described the role of improper association of ideas in mental illness (Locke, 1690/1976). David Hume added cause and effect (contiguity in time) as a law of association (Hume, 1739/2007). Pavlov explored the mechanisms of association empirically (Pavlov, 1927). His conditioning paradigms highlighted that mere contiguity is not sufficient for learning. For example, Leon Kamin discovered blocking, which involves the retardation of learning about a novel cue-outcome association when that cue is paired with a stimulus that already predicts the outcome – the pre-trained cue blocks learning about the novel cue (Kamin, 1969). Blocking demands that the association of ideas is sensitive to surprise (McLaren & Dickinson, 1990).

Widrow and Hoff created a simple connectionist neural network of nodes, representing inputs and outputs as links between nodes (Widrow & Hoff, 1960). Those links were strengthened by reducing an error signal, the mismatch between the desired output from a given input and the output that actually occurred. A similar algorithm was proposed for animal conditioning by Rescorla and Wagner (Rescorla & Wagner, 1972); environmental stimuli induce expectations about subsequent states of the world, exciting representations of those states. Any mismatch between the expectancies and actual experience is a PE. PEs are used as teaching signals to update future expectancies about stimuli and states. Under this scheme, blocking occurs because the outcome of the compound of pre-trained and novel cues is completely predicted, by the pre-trained cue, which precludes the generation of prediction error signal and, subsequently, learning about the association between the novel cue and the outcome. Consequently, a greater magnitude PE should weaken blocking. This has been demonstrated with amphetamine administration in experimental animals (O'Tuathaigh et al., 2003), chemogenetic manipulations of cingulate cortex in rats (Yau & McNally, 2015) and optogenetic manipulation of dopamine neurons in mice (Steinberg et al., 2013). In humans, weaker blocking has been observed in patients with schizophrenia (Moran, Al-Uzri, Watson, & Reveley, 2003) and the extent to which the neural PE signal is inappropriately engaged correlates with delusion-like beliefs (Corlett & Fletcher, 2012).

Attention is also critical for associative learning. Cues that are predictably associated with important outcomes are allocated most attention, and thus more readily enter associative relationships (Mackintosh, 1975). However, stimuli with an uncertain predictive history also garner attention (Pearce & Hall, 1980). Clearly attention is important to association formation in different ways under different circumstances. One crucial circumstance involves reward prediction; stimuli garner incentive salience to the extent that they drive goal-directed action (Robinson & Berridge, 2001). We must recognize the important impact of Kapur's perspicuous incentive salience theory of psychosis (Kapur, 2003), that delusions form as a consequence of aberrant incentive salience driven by an excess of dopamine in the ventral striatum. We note though that it was presaged by more mechanistic theories grounded in associative learning theory (Gray et al., 1991; Miller, 1976), it did not readily explain the role of other neurotransmitters like glutamate and that the data on dopamine release capacity (Howes et al., 2009) have implicated the associative striatum (not the ventral striatum) in the genesis of psychosis. Nevertheless, there do seem to be phenomenological and empirical data linking the broad category of salient events to delusions.

How do we reconcile salience and associative learning accounts with the phenomenology and neurobiology of psychosis? Bayesian models have been invoked to explain both associative learning and psychosis (Corlett, Frith & Fletcher, 2009; Corlett et al., 2010).

2.3 Bayesian Minds and Brains

Thomas Bayes was a British clergyman and mathematician whose theorem was published posthumously. His is a theorem of conditional probabilities, of event A given event B, expressed as follows:

$$P(A_i \mid B) = \frac{P(\mathrm{A_i})P(\mathrm{B} \mid A_i)}{\sum_{j=1}^{k} P(\mathrm{A_j})P(\mathrm{B} \mid A_j)}$$

Bayes may offer a way of bridging levels of explanation – from single neurons, to groups of cells, to systems, and ultimately associative learning and belief (Clark, 2013).

Bayesian Brains Are Predictive Brains

Under this account of brain function, organisms have a brain to anticipate future situations, thus enabling survival by maximizing rewards and minimizing punishments. This is achieved computationally by making predictions and minimizing prediction errors through the hierarchical anatomy of the brain – wherein predictions are communicated in a top-down fashion, from higher to lower layers. When predictions encounter bottom-up sensory information that does not match – prediction errors are generated which are either accommodated (ignored) or assimilated (incorporated into future predictions).

Predictions originate in areas columns with less laminar differentiation (e.g. agranular cortex) and are propagated to areas with greater laminar differentiation (such as granular cortex). In the prototypical case, prediction signals originate in the deep layers (primarily layer V) and terminate in the supragranular division of dysgranular and granular regions — principally on dendrites in layer I, as well as on neurons in layers II and III.

Predictions then change the firing rates of neurons in layers I–III in anticipation of thalamic input. If the pattern of firing in a cortical column sufficiently anticipates the afferent thalamic input, there will be little or no prediction error. However, a mismatch will entail a prediction error. Some pyramidal neurons within a cortical column function as precision units that dynamically modify the gain on neurons that compute prediction error. Precision units modulate the weight of prediction errors on the basis of the relative confidence in the descending predictions compared to incoming sensory signals.

Chanes and Feldman Barrett applied this analysis more broadly to agranular cortices, notably to the limbic regions that regulate visceral control of the body's internal milieu. Regions including the ACC, insula and thalamus may compute predictions and prediction errors and then other higher and lower cortical regions represent the specific domains being computed. We believe these sorts of models will guide prediction, inference and interpretation of neural data gathered during the formation and operation of beliefs. This arrangement may allow for the encapsulation of beliefs, without having to postulate a modular mental organization (see below).

The specific path the information takes is governed by the relative precision of the priors, as well as prediction errors (Adams et al., 2013). As Körding and Wolpert (2004) showed, the relative precision that governs how strongly we will rely on incoming data can be expressed as a linear function of priors and likelihood (probability of observing the data we see if the prior was true)[1]:

$$E(Posterior) \propto (1 - r_{reliance}) * Prior + r_{reliance} * Likelihood$$

[1]We are assuming that both the distribution of priors and likelihood is Gaussian, with $\varepsilon_{prior} \sim N(\mu, \sigma^2_{prior})$ and $\varepsilon_{likelihood} \sim N(\mu, \sigma^2_{likelihood})$.

If the pool of our priors is both large and heterogeneous, the incoming data will play an important role in influencing our prediction. But if our priors are precise it will have a negligible role in updating.

Dopamine, serotonin and acetylcholine may code the precision of priors and prediction errors in separate hierarchies (Marshall et al., 2016). For example, acetylcholine is involved in specifying the precision of perceptual priors. However, stimulating dopamine neurons in the VTA, drives acetylcholine release in the nucleus basalis, which expands the cortical representation of sensory stimuli that coincide with the stimulation (Bao, Chan, & Merzenich, 2001). This could be a mechanism through which salient events garner greater cortical representation.

The importance of the element of surprise in the learning process has long been appreciated. C. S. Pierce coined the term abduction as a key aspect of his explanation of inference. He dissociated abduction from other mechanisms of explanation like deduction and induction (Peirce, 1931–58). Abductive inference has been used to help describe the generation of explanations for distorted perception culminating in delusions (Coltheart, Menzies, & Sutton, 2010).

Capgras syndrome is one of the most rare neurological delusions: (Capgras & Reboul-Lachaux, 1923). Here, an individual, sees his loved ones as imposters.

The confusion that accompanies living with this feeling of ongoing strangeness could become exhausting – a clear explanation, like "that's actually not my wife" – may be protective, although far from comforting.

Kihlstrom and Hoyt (1988) have discussed the explanation process as it might pertain to misconstrued experiences. They appealed to a number of heuristics and biases to which healthy people are susceptible discussed at length by Kahneman, Slovic, and Tversky (1982).

Kihlstrom and Hoyt (1988) describe a man, walking down the street minding his own business, who suddenly and unexpectedly has an anomalous experience – he hears his name perhaps or perhaps a strange or unpleasant thought crosses his mind. All he knows is that something unusual just happened to him. The person then will initiate a search for the cause of an event; people seem to have a general propensity towards causal explanation (Michotte, 1963), and anomalous schema and incongruent events demand such explanation.

Bayesian Biases?

The Bayesian approach can be used to formalize several well-studied belief biases. For example, we know that providing people with counterarguments that undermine their beliefs is not only insufficient, but it can also ironically enhance their confidence in these beliefs – just like the Seekers in the millennial cult.

The cognitive psychology of explanation involves conscious deliberative processes; our models of delusions, perception, and learning are not committed to a requirement for conscious processing. While some associative learning effects require subjects to be aware of contingencies (Shanks & Channon, 2002), there are examples of prediction error-driven learning about stimuli that were presented subliminally (Pessiglione et al., 2008). Helmholtz considered perception to be a process of unconscious inference over alternate hypotheses about the causes of sensory stimulation (von Helmholtz, 1878/1971). Fleminger applied this reasoning to misidentification delusions, arguing that misidentification of familiar perceptual objects and scenes was due to a dysfunction in the pre-conscious specification of perceptual predictions (Fleminger, 1992) that would engender a prediction error demanding explanation.

Psychotic illnesses like schizophrenia are associated with resistance to perceptual illusions (Dima et al., 2009). It seems that in patients with delusions, perceptual priors are more flexible and prone to change, and therefore less likely to affect perception. However, extra-perceptual priors, may be stronger. A team lead by Paul Fletcher (Teufel et al., 2015) recently showed that it is this extra perceptual knowledge sphere, where recent prior experience can change subsequent processing, which is hyper-engaged in individuals prone to schizophrenia and correlates with their symptom severity.

Perhaps most relevant to the present discussion is confirmation bias (Lord et al., 1979; Nickerson, 1998), through which prior beliefs bias current decision-making. More specifically, contradictory data are ignored if they violate a cherished hypothesis. Prediction error-driven learning models have been generated that instantiate a confirmation bias. According to theoretical (Grossberg, 2000) and quantitative computational models (Doll, Jacobs, Sanfey, & Frank, 2009), confirmation biases favor learning that conforms to beliefs through the top-down influence of the frontal cortex on striatal prediction error learning. DARPP-32 and DRD2 are two striatally enriched proteins. DARPP-32 – an intracellular signaling nexus, DRD2 a key component of dopamine D2 receptors. Both proteins are involved in prediction error signaling (Frank, Moustafa, Haughey, Curran, & Hutchison, 2007; Heyser, Fienberg, Greengard, & Gold, 2000) and involved in the top-down cancellation of striatal positive and negative prediction error signals that conflict with prior beliefs. Using a behavioral neurogenetic approach, Doll and colleagues (2009) found that genes for DARPP-32 and DRD2.

Of special interest to this discussion, confirmation bias is increased in individuals with delusions (Balzan, Delfabbro, Galletly, & Woodward, 2013). Also, DARPP-32 has been implicated in the genetic risk for schizophrenia, the effects of psychotomimetic drugs (Svenningsson et al., 2003), learning changes in instrumental contingencies (Heyser et al., 2000), as well as the functional and structural coupling between frontal cortex and striatum (Meyer-Lindenberg et al., 2007). On the other hand, Doll and colleagues (2014) found that patients with chronic schizophrenia did not show an enhanced fronto-striatal confirmation bias. Furthermore, it is possible that confirmation biases are specific to delusion contents (encapsulated) rather than a general deficit (Balzan et al., 2013).

People attribute causal significance to the most salient perceptual elements co-occurring with the event to be explained (Taylor & Fiske, 1978). In the terms of associative theories, aberrant prediction error signals might randomly increase the attentional salience of aspects of the perceptual field, leading subjects to attribute inappropriate importance to irrelevant features of the environment (Beninger & Miller, 1998; Gray, 1993, 1998a, 1998b; Gray, Feldon, Rawlins, Hemsley, & Smith, 1991; Hemsley, 1993, 2005; Kapur, 2003, 2004; Kapur, Mizrahi, & Li, 2005; Miller, 1993).

People tend to jump to conclusions, employing short cuts and heuristics. For example, people assume that the features of a causal event should resemble the features of its outcome. Unpleasant effects should have unpleasant causes. Furthermore, peoples' causal judgments tend to be greatly influenced by their *a priori* theories about causation: If someone has the idea that many unpleasant events in the outside world reflect the activities of an international terrorist conspiracy, those same terrorists may be held responsible for unpleasant internal events as well. It seems possible to appeal to an associative mechanism to explain this heuristic, a particular personal bias may be mediated by associations; the increased salience of a particular out-group may increase the propensity to form associations between that group and events in the environment.

The availability heuristic posits that the basis for judgment is the ease with which a plausible scenario can be constructed mentally. Judgments of causality are affected by the ease with which the person can imagine a path from a presumed cause to a known effect. When unpredicted events occur, the simulation process traces causal links back to prior causes. Consider a psychotic patient searching the environment for a likely cause of their anomalous experiences (Kihlstrom & Hoyt, 1988). Salient objects and events – a honk or a wave from a passing driver, perhaps a member of a minority group standing on a street corner – will inevitably draw attention and be given special weight as a likely cause of their troublesome internal events. If there is nothing perceptually salient, events may be retrieved from memory – a curse uttered in anger by a co-worker (Kihlstrom & Hoyt, 1988). If no suitable cause is generated through perception or memory, the simulation process may be invoked (Kihlstrom & Hoyt, 1988). The person may imagine possible causes and grasp the first one that comes to mind as the most likely explanation (Kihlstrom & Hoyt, 1988; Maher, 1974, 1988a, 1988b).

It is plausible that the simulation heuristic may be mediated by associative mechanisms, namely the retrieval of associative chains such that the individual can mentally trace the associations from outcome to cause. A probability tree-search mechanism mediated by prefrontal cortex may underpin this heuristic (Daw, Niv, & Dayan, 2005). Under the influence of aberrant subcortical prediction error signals, this mechanism may be invoked to account for the apparent relatedness of stimuli and events or the aberrant attentional salience of previously irrelevant background stimuli (Kihlstrom & Hoyt, 1988).

While the heuristics described so far are involved in the initial generation of a causal explanation, anchoring and adjustment might be involved in the maintenance of delusional beliefs. Many judgments begin as hypotheses – tentative conclusions that can be revised on the basis of newly acquired evidence. However, it has long been appreciated that final judgments are inordinately influenced by first impressions: The initial judgment serves as an anchor for the final one, and there is very little subsequent adjustment. The anchoring and adjustment heuristic reflects a general tendency to rely on initial or partial judgments, giving too little weight to newly acquired information. By virtue of its use, judgments of causality tend not to accommodate new information that should instigate revision. Instead, knowledge gained subsequent to the initial judgment may be distorted so as to fit the original causal theory. Subjects thus adopt suboptimal verificationist strategies, seeking and paying special attention to information that is consistent with their hypothesis (Snyder & Swann, 1978). As many researchers will attest, when confronted with evidence that counters a cherished belief, individuals often react by challenging the evidence (Bentall, Corcoran, Howard, Blackwood, & Kinderman, 2001). Once an explanation for odd perceptual and attentional phenomena is arrived at, the patient experiences relief from anxiety. The experience of insight relief diminishes the person's subsequent motivation to question his or her original conclusions and increases resistance to contrary information. This theme is represented in Miller's (1993) associative learning based account of psychosis. He argues that arriving at a causal explanation that accounts for aberrant experiences is so rewarding/relieving that it is accompanied by a surge of dopamine (Miller, 1993). Dopamine also has impacts on the consolidation of memories (Dalley et al., 2005), and as such, an incorrect conclusion may be "stamped-in" to long-term memory by dopamine, rendering it relatively impervious to disconfirmatory evidence.

The anchoring and adjustment heuristic may relate to another prominent cognitive theory of delusional belief formation, the "jumping to conclusions bias" (Garety, Hemsley, & Wessely, 1991; Hemsley & Garety, 1986; Huq, Garety, & Hemsley, 1988). This bias was well-documented in healthy subjects (Asch, 1946; Kahneman, 2011), where individuals tend to make decisions hastily, and on the basis of little evidence. But the bulk of empirical evidence for this account comes from investigations of clinical patients' performance on probabilistic reasoning tasks; typically, participants are presented with two jars holding colored beads in different proportions. The jars are removed from view and subjects are presented with beads, drawn one at a time from a jar, and patients are then asked to predict which jar the beads are coming. Individuals with delusions tend to make a decision after only one bead (Fear & Healy, 1997; Garety et al., 1991; Huq et al., 1988; Moritz & Woodward, 2005). It is important to note that the bias is not specific to individuals with delusions (Menon, Pomarol-Clotet, McKenna, & McCarthy, 2006) and may represent a desire to end cognitive testing more rapidly or to avoid uncertain experiences (Moutoussis, Bentall, El-Deredy, & Dayan, 2011). Hence, this bias may also pertain to the defensive functions of beliefs (protecting against low self-esteem resulting from poor cognitive performance and the toxic effects of uncertainty).

The jumping to conclusions bias may represent a need for closure (McKay, Langdon, & Coltheart, 2006) in the face of aberrant prediction error signals that engender a stressful state of uncertainty about the world.

Recent behavioral and neuroimaging data suggest that as uncertainty increases, so do learning rates (Behrens, Hunt, Woolrich, & Rushworth, 2008; Pearce & Hall, 1980). When non-delusional healthy subjects jump to conclusions (updating their beliefs extensively after one trial in conditions of high uncertainty), there is hyper-connectivity between the ventrolateral prefrontal cortex and hippocampus functional magnetic resonance signals (Lee, O'Doherty, & Shimojo, 2015).

Moritz and Woodward suggest that a liberal acceptance bias might account for apparent jumping to conclusions. When only two mutually exclusive options are available (as in the beads task), individuals rapidly *accept* that the beads are coming from a particular jar, but they do not *decide* that they are to the exclusion of other possibilities (Moritz & Woodward, 2005). This account allows for over-adjustment following contradictory evidence, since although they have strongly accepted one conclusion (the beads are from one jar), they do not exclude the alternative conclusion (that the beads are coming from the other jar).

When given more than two alternatives (for example in a thematic apperception task, where participants are shown pictures and asked to rate the plausibility of particular interpretations), psychotic patients entertain a broader range of possible interpretations (rating multiple alternatives as excellent or good interpretations of a particular scenario), whereas healthy participants are more cautious and effectively narrow down the set of possible alternatives. The broadening of plausible explanations may be a manifestation of Miller's inappropriate relatedness of entities (Miller, 1976, 1993). And while it can undoubtedly minimize the rigidity with which one may hold on to an explanation, when new information arrives, at a higher, representational level, it may lead to the entertainment of implausible or absurd accounts for a particular set of circumstances.

Since anomalous perceptual and attentional experiences may be unpleasant (Maher, 1974, 1988b), it is important to consider the biases that distort causal judgments about negatively valenced events. For example, when humans make causal attributions, they tend to fall for benefactance bias, such that they internalize the cause of positive events and externally attribute negatively valenced events (Greenwald, 1980; Kaney & Bentall, 1992). Such *Lake Woebegone Effects* – where everyone is smarter and more beautiful than average – are exaggerated in patients with paranoia (Kaney & Bentall, 1992). Hence a psychotic individual seeking an explanation for their unpleasant anomalous experiences will most often look to the environment outside them, rather than say, to a dysfunction in their own brain or body. These biases were the only types of belief afforded the status of adaptive misbeliefs by McKay and Dennett (2009). If these biases may be related to delusions, perhaps then, certain delusions could be adaptive misbeliefs.

In an fMRI study of the self-serving hindsight bias in healthy individuals, subjects silently read sentences describing positively and negatively valenced social events, then imagined the event happening to them, and finally decided the cause of the event, whether internal (was it something about you?) or external (was it something about your friend? was it something about the situation or circumstances?). Self-serving biased attributions (internal attribution of positive and external attribution of negative events) were associated with striatal activation (Blackwood et al., 2003), previously implicated in the motivational control of behavior (Robbins & Everitt, 1996), as well as in the mediation of delusions (Laruelle, Abi-Dargham, Gil, Kegeles, & Innis, 1999). Menon and colleagues (2011) showed that delusions of reference were associated with inappropriate striatal engagement during reading of sentences that were inappropriately judged to be self-related.

2.4 Delusions, Self and Others

Thus far, we have discussed beliefs in the context of individuals. However, they are constructed in a social context that involves interacting with others and engaging with their perspectives. In our theory, the brain models incoming data and minimizes prediction error (Friston & Kiebel, 2009). However, it also actively samples those data, by performing actions on the world (e.g. moving through it) (Friston, Daunizeau, Kilner, & Kiebel, 2010). By predicting (and ignoring) the sensory consequences of our actions we also model ourselves as agents that exist. And, by identifying with the top layers of the hierarchy, the conscious experience of being that self emerges (Blanke & Metzinger, 2009).

Passivity experiences – the sense that ones' actions are under external control – may arise when the predictive modeling of one's actions fails and the active sampling of sensory data becomes noisy (Stephan, Friston, & Frith, 2009). In such circumstances thoughts and actions that were self-generated are not attributed to self and, at the extremes, one no longer identifies with ones' hierarchical model of the world. On the other hand, paranoia and referential delusions may be associated with excessive responsibility, our sense of self extends to areas it should not.

Ketamine augments experience of the rubber hand illusion, the spurious sense of ownership of a prop-hand if the hand is stroked at the same time as one's own hand (Morgan et al., 2011). People on ketamine get the illusion more strongly and they experience it even in a control condition when the real and rubber hands are stroked asynchronously (Morgan et al., 2011). Patients with schizophrenia (Peled, Pressman, Geva, & Modai, 2003) and chronic ketamine abusers show the same excessive experience of the illusion, in the synchronous and asynchronous conditions (Tang et al., 2015). Activity in the right anterior insula cortex increases to the extent that individuals experience the illusion. Anil Seth and others have argued that the anterior insula is a key nexus for the PE driven inferences that guide perceptions of bodily ownership and agency (Palmer, Seth, & Hohwy, 2015; Seth, 2013; Seth, Suzuki, & Critchley, 2011). Others highlight the parietal cortex as a key locus for the illusion (Ehrsson, Holmes, & Passingham, 2005).

2.5 Blankets, Brains, Beliefs

The ***"Markov blanket"*** might be one means a Bayesian brain distinguishes self and others (Friston & Frith, 2015). A Markov blanket it like a cell membrane. It shields the interior of the cell from direct exposure to the conditions outside it, but it contains sufficient information (in the form of actual and potential structures) for the cell to be influenced by and to influence those external conditions. The Markov blanket of "an animal" encloses the Markov blankets of "the organs," which enclose the Markov blanket of "their cells," which enclose the Markov blankets of "their nuclei," etc. To distinguish such levels of hierarchies, Pearl used the terms "parents" and "children." The Markov blanket for a node in a Bayesian network is the set of nodes composed of its parents, its children, and its children's other parents. The Markov blanket of a node contains all the variables that shield the node from the rest of the network. This means that the Markov blanket of a node is the only knowledge required to predict the behavior of the node.

A Markov blanket separates states into *internal* and *external.* External states are hidden (insulated) from the internal states. In other words, from the node's, or individual's perspective, the external states can be seen only indirectly by the internal states, via the Markov blanket. The internal state models (learns and make inferences about) the external, lying on the other side of the blanket.

Despite serving as a boundary, the Markov blanket may also have a role in synchronizing self with others. This occurs, for example, when we speak to another agent. In our predictive coding scheme, we adapt language comprehension to the demands of any given communicative situation, estimating the precision of our prior beliefs at a given representational level and the reliability of new inputs to that level (Friston & Frith, 2015).

In a hermeneutic setting, though, Bayesian brains do not predict each other; they predict themselves provided those predictions are enacted. The enactment of sensory (proprioceptive) predictions is a tenet of active inference, as we can minimize prediction errors by actively sampling data that conform to our predictions (Friston & Frith, 2015). This framework for communication is inherently embodied and enactive in nature.

The internal states (of each agent) and external states (their partner) – and the Markov blanket that separates them – possess something called a random dynamical attractor that mediates the synchrony (Friston, Sengupta, & Auletta, 2014). Through this attractor, the external and internal states track each other, or the states one agent occupies impose constraints on states the other can occupy. However, if the Markov blanket or attractor become dysfunctional, first rank psychotic symptoms (Schneider, 1957) may result. That is, you may hear voices from recognizable social agents that communicate with you, or believe that your thoughts, actions, and emotions have been inserted into your mind by others.

Of particular relevance is the implication of temporoparietal junction in hearing voices. According to Saxe, this is a central role in representing others' mental states through predictive coding (Koster-Hale & Saxe, 2013). Stimulating temporoparietal junction induces a "sensed presence." Taken together with theories that suggest that hallucinations and delusions arise when reality monitoring (or more accurately reality filtering) fails such that inner speech is confused with external speech (Johnson & Raye, 1981), one can see how perturbations of these inferential mechanisms could render inner speech experienced as the communicative intent of an external agent. Similarly, Fernyhough, after Vygotsky, argues that children learn language through interaction with others; this begins out loud and later when we internalize speech as thought aberrations of this process subtend an inner voice that does not belong and is rather another agent (Jones & Fernyhough, 2007). Predictive social models may also be set awry by poor attachment (Fineberg, Steinfeld, Brewer, & Corlett, 2014).

2.6 Therapeutic Implications

Predictive coding seems to entail learning about different contingencies: low-level contingencies, detected within a perceptual module (e.g. V1 or A1) and higher-level contingencies that involve integrating across time, space, and sensory modalities. When low-level contingency detection fails, higher-level, top-down knowledge-based contingency detection compensates – hence a stronger reliance on high-level priors as Teufel et al. (2015) observed in people at risk for psychosis. To reinforce this idea, we point to a phenomenon from social psychology – lack of personal control. Remembering a time in one's life when one lacked control, such as preparing to skydive from an airplane, triggers a compensatory increase in illusory pattern perception like superstitious behavior and belief in conspiracy theories; there needn't necessarily be a direct connection between uncertainty and the way in which it is compensated (Proulx, Inzlicht, & Harmon-Jones, 2012), as any belief will do. Ultimately, this conception of belief underlines our aversion to uncertainty and our preference for reasons and explanations.

Why beliefs backfire in response to challenges is not yet fully understood, however, there are models of the political polarization of beliefs in response to the same evidence that suggest the strength of priors are important. If priors are strong, polarizing effects are more likely. Personally relevant priors that contribute to self-identity are likely to be the strongest. This is not encouraging with regard to efforts to change strong beliefs.

However, there are some encouraging new data. One promising line of inquiry, with respect to vaccine beliefs, is the involvement of individuals who used to object to vaccines and have now changed their minds in engaging with others who are against vaccinations (Brendan Nyhan, *personal communication*). Many researchers agree delusions and beliefs are often grounded in personal experiences. To the credulous, personal experiences are a reliable source. Relinquishing those beliefs on the basis of others' testimony is strongly related to the credibility of the source (Nyhan & Reifler, 2013); for example, do the individuals trying to change another's mind have a vested reason to disagree, like professional status, roles, or affiliations? Perhaps large-scale anti-stigma educational activities in mental health have failed because they did not employ individuals with lived experience to spread the word about mental illness (Corrigan, 2012). With regard to fixed and distressing delusional beliefs, perhaps peer-support might supplement our standard approaches to mollifying delusions. People with lived experience who have recovered from delusions or learned how to manage them might be better at helping their peers experiencing ongoing delusions. More direct methods might involve hearing the story and imagining the position of someone directly affected by the belief. This technique was tested for beliefs about transgendered individuals with success (Broockman & Kalla, 2016). With regards to the putative circuit, perhaps engaging empathy in this manner permits assimilation and belief updating rather than the discarding of prediction error.

2.7 What Shape Is the Mind?

There are of course other theories of beliefs and delusions. Extant cognitive neuropsychiatric (Halligan & David, 2001) explanations of delusions range from single factor (Maher, 1974), to two-factor to interactionist. The single factor account appeals to a deficit in perception; the delusion formation process being a logical consequence of such an unsettling experience (Maher, 1974, 1988a). Two-factor theorists appeal to a deficit in familiarity processing with an additional dysfunction in belief evaluation such that the unlikely explanation ("My loved one has been replaced") is favored (Coltheart, 2010; Coltheart, Langdon, & McKay, 2007; Mendoza, 1978).

Two-factor theory is attractive in its simplicity. It derives from cognitive neuropsychology; the consideration of patients who develop delusions following brain damage (Coltheart, 2010; Coltheart & Davies, 2000; Coltheart, Langdon, & McKay, 2010). It holds that two factors are necessary for delusions; a perceptual dysfunction and a belief evaluation dysfunction. Each is attributable to separate locations of brain damage – for Capgras delusion the perceptual dysfunction may involve ventromedial prefrontal cortex damage that renders familiar faces unfamiliar. However, people with this damage do not always have Capgras (Tranel & Damasio, 1985). Coltheart and others posit that a further deficit in belief evaluation is necessary for the delusion. They suggest right dorsolateral prefrontal cortex may be the locus of the second factor (Coltheart, 2010; Coltheart & Davies, 2000; Coltheart, Langdon, et al., 2010). The logic here is flawed; a second factor is only suggested. It would be necessitated by a double dissociation of functions (Coltheart, 2002). The data here are still consistent with a single factor: The ventromedial perceptual dysfunction could occur to a greater or lesser degree, delusions could arise in those patients who have more extensive damage and they may be absent in people with less extensive damage. Nevertheless, two factor theories emphasized the role of perception and belief in the genesis of psychotic symptoms. Updated versions of the theory implicated Bayesian mechanisms of belief evaluation in delusion formation (Coltheart, Menzies, et al., 2010) and interactive models suggest that perception and belief intersect in a Bayesian manner that may become deranged when delusions form (Young, 2008). This update moves two-factor theory nearer to PE theory.

However, PE theory challenges the strict distinction between perception and belief, and therefore the necessity for two factors to explain delusions (Powers, Kelley, & Corlett 2016). The disagreement is not about delusions per se, but rather cognitive neuropsychology more broadly, the shape of the mind, the allowable relationships between processes and how one ought to relate the mind with the brain. These may seem arcane. However, we try to explain delusions to better treat them. Understanding their component cognitive and neural mechanisms is essential.

Modularity Versus Penetrability

In *The Modularity of Mind* (1983), Fodor sketched a mental architecture comprised of modules—systems that process a single specific kind of information (Fodor, 1983). 2-factor theory demands this encapsulated modularity. Belief and perception are separate and can be damaged independently. Information flows from perception to belief and never in the opposite direction (Fotopoulou, 2014). An encapsulated perceptual system, kept separate from the influence of beliefs, could keep our beliefs grounded in the truth offered by our senses (Quine & Quine, 1951). However, a cognitively penetrable perceptual apparatus, per PE theory, may be equally adaptive, despite misperceiving and misbelieving (Johnson & Fowler, 2011; McKay & Dennett, 2009). We perceive what would need to be present in order for our sensations to make sense, not necessarily what is actually there (von Helmholtz, 1867; Hume, 1900). Predictive perception is penetrated by beliefs to the extent this minimizes overall long-term PE (Lupyan & Clark, 2015).

Ultimately, the two explanations (two-factor and predictive processing) are cast at different explanatory levels. Two-factor theory is concerned with describing cognitive architectures. Predictive processing aims to unite brain, behavioral and phenomenological data for all delusions (neurological and those that occur in schizophrenia) as well as other psychotic symptoms like hallucinations and a-motivation.

2.8 Conclusion

A better understanding of delusions may be achieved by taking a reductionist approach to beliefs, conceiving of them as learned associations between representations that govern perception (both internal and external) and action. Central to the process of associative belief formation is PE; the mismatch between prior expectation and current circumstances. Depending on the precision (or inverse variance) of the PE (relative to the prior), it may drive new learning – updating of the belief, or it may be disregarded. We have argued that this process of PE signaling and accommodation/assimilation may be awry in people with psychotic illnesses. In particular, we believe delusions form when PE is signaled inappropriately with high precision, such that it garners new and aberrant learning. We have described animal research that has furnished a mechanistic understanding of PE signaling in terms of underlying neurobiology; glutamatergic mechanisms underlie the specification of PE (NMDA receptors signal top-down expectancies, AMPA the feedforward error signal), and, depending on the specific hierarchy, slower neuromodulators (like dopamine, acetylcholine, serotonin, noradrenaline and oxytocin) signal precision of priors and PE. There are thus many routes through which PE can be aberrantly signaled and many heterogeneous consequences of aberrant PE. The inferences that are perturbed give rise to the specific contents of delusions (they are about other people and one's relationships to them, because these are the hardest inferences to make). We have described how such error correcting inferential mechanisms might give rise to the sense of bodily agency (the sense of being a self) and to a sense of reality more broadly. Disrupting these senses is profoundly distressing and results in psychosis. Armed with an understanding of exactly how people with delusions fare on these tasks and exactly which neural mechanisms underpin them, we will be much better placed to determine the pathophysiology underpinning delusions and to tailor treatment approaches aimed at that pathophysiology.

REFERENCES

Adams, R. A., Stephan, K. E., Brown, H. R., Frith, C. D., & Friston, K. J. (2013). The computational anatomy of psychosis. *Frontiers in Psychiatry, 4*, 47. https://doi.org/10.3389/fpsyt.2013.00047

Arbib, M., & Bota, M. (2003). Language evolution: neural homologies and neuroinformatics. *Neural Networks, 16*(9), 1237–1260. https://doi.org/10.1016/j.neunet.2003.08.002

Arbib, M. A. (2005). From monkey-like action recognition to human language: An evolutionary framework for neurolinguistics. *The Behavioral and Brain Sciences, 28*(2), 105–124 discussion 125-167.

Aristotle. (Ed.). (350 B.C./1930). *On Memory and Reminiscence* (Vol. 3). Oxford, UK: Clarendon Press.

Asch, S. E. (1946). Forming impressions of personality. *Journal of Abnormal and Social Psychology, 41*(3), 258–290.

Balzan, R., Delfabbro, P., Galletly, C., & Woodward, T. (2013). Confirmation biases across the psychosis continuum: The contribution of hypersalient evidence-hypothesis matches. *The British Journal of Clinical Psychology/The British Psychological Society, 52*(1), 53–69. https://doi.org/10.1111/bjc.12000

Bao, S., Chan, V. T., & Merzenich, M. M. (2001). Cortical remodelling induced by activity of ventral tegmental dopamine neurons. *Nature, 412*(6842), 79–83. https://doi.org/10.1038/35083586

Behrens, T. E., Hunt, L. T., Woolrich, M. W., & Rushworth, M. F. (2008). Associative learning of social value. *Nature, 456*(7219), 245–249. https://doi.org/10.1038/nature07538

Beninger, R. J., & Miller, R. (1998). Dopamine D1-like receptors and reward-related incentive learning. *Neuroscience and Biobehavioral Reviews, 22*(2), 335–345.

Bentall, R. P., Corcoran, R., Howard, R., Blackwood, N., & Kinderman, P. (2001). Persecutory delusions: A review and theoretical integration. *Clinical Psychology Review, 21*(8), 1143–1192.

Blackwood, N. J., Bentall, R. P., Ffytche, D. H., Simmons, A., Murray, R. M., & Howard, R. J. (2003). Self-responsibility and the self-serving bias: An fMRI investigation of causal attributions. *NeuroImage, 20*(2), 1076–1085. https://doi.org/10.1016/S1053-8119(03)00331-8

Blanke, O., & Metzinger, T. (2009). Full-body illusions and minimal phenomenal selfhood. *Trends in Cognitive Sciences, 13*(1), 7–13. https://doi.org/10.1016/j.tics.2008.10.003

Broockman, D., & Kalla, J. (2016). Durably reducing transphobia: A field experiment on door-to-door canvassing. *Science, 352*(6282), 220–224. https://doi.org/10.1126/science.aad9713

Brown, M., & Kuperberg, G. R. (2015). A hierarchical generative framework of language processing: Linking language perception, interpretation, and production abnormalities in schizophrenia. *Frontiers in Human Neuroscience, 9*, 643. https://doi.org/10.3389/fnhum.2015.00643

Capgras, J., & Reboul-Lachaux, J. (1923). L'illusion des 'sosies' dans un de!lire syste!matise chronique. *Bulletin de la Société clinique de médecine mentale, 2*, 6–16.

Chawke, C., & Kanai, R. (2016). Alteration of political belief by non-invasive brain stimulation. *Frontiers in Human Neuroscience, 9*, 621.

Clark, A. (2013). Whatever next? Predictive brains, situated agents, and the future of cognitive science. *The Behavioral and Brain Sciences, 36*(3), 181–204. https://doi.org/10.1017/S0140525X12000477

Coltheart, M. (2002). Cognitive neuropsychology. In H. Pashler & J. Wixted (Eds.), *Steven's handbook of experimental psychology* (Vol. 4, 3rd ed.). Hoboken, NJ: Wiley.

Coltheart, M. (2010). The neuropsychology of delusions. *Annals of the New York Academy of Sciences, 1191*(1), 16–26. doi:NYAS5496 [pii] https://doi.org/10.1111/j.1749-6632.2010.05496.x.

Coltheart, M., Cox, R., Sowman, P., Morgan, H., Barnier, A., Langdon, R., … Polito, V. (2018). Belief, delusion, hypnosis, and the right dorsolateral prefrontal cortex: A transcranial magnetic stimulation study. *Cortex*. https://doi.org/10.1016/j.cortex.2018.01.001

Coltheart, M., & Davies, M. (2000). *Pathologies of belief*. Oxford, UK: Blackwell.

Coltheart, M., Langdon, R., & McKay, R. (2007). Schizophrenia and monothematic delusions. *Schizophrenia Bulletin, 33*(3), 642–647.

Coltheart, M., Langdon, R., & McKay, R. (2010). Delusional Belief. *Annual Review of Psychology*. https://doi.org/10.1146/annurev.psych.121208.131622

Coltheart, M., Menzies, P., & Sutton, J. (2010). Abductive inference and delusional belief. *Cognitive Neuropsychiatry, 15*(1), 261–287. https://doi.org/10.1080/13546800903439120

Corlett, P. R. (2015). Answering some phenomenal challenges to the prediction error model of delusions. *World Psychiatry, 14*(2), 181–183. https://doi.org/10.1002/wps.20211

Corlett, P. R., Aitken, M. R. F., Dickinson, A., Shanks, D. R., Honey, G. D., Honey, R. A. E., … Fletcher, P. C. (2004). Prediction error during retrospective revaluation of causal associations in humans: fMRI evidence in favor of an associative model of learning. *Neuron, 44*(5), 877. https://doi.org/10.1016/j.neuron.2004.11.022

Corlett, P. R., & Fletcher, P. C. (2012). The neurobiology of schizotypy: Fronto-striatal prediction error signal correlates with delusion-like beliefs in healthy people. *Neuropsychologia, 50*(14), 3612–3620. https://doi.org/10.1016/j.neuropsychologia.2012.09.045

Corlett, P. R., & Fletcher, P. C. (2014). Computational psychiatry: A Rosetta Stone linking the brain to mental illness. *Lancet Psychiatry, 1*, 399.

Corlett, P. R., Frith, C. D., & Fletcher, P. C. (2009a). From drugs to deprivation: A Bayesian framework for understanding models of psychosis. *Psychopharmacology, 206*(4), 515–530.

Corlett, P. R., Frith, C. D., & Fletcher, P. C. (2009b). *From drugs to deprivation: A Bayesian framework for understanding models of psychosis* (Vol. 206, pp. 515–530). Berlin/Heidelberg, Germany: Springer Science & Business Media.

Corlett, P. R., Honey, G. D., & Fletcher, P. C. (2007). From prediction error to psychosis: Ketamine as a pharmacological model of delusions. *Journal of Psychopharmacology, 21*(3), 238–252. https://doi.org/10.1177/0269881107077716

Corlett, P. R., Honey, G. D., Krystal, J. H., & Fletcher, P. C. (2010). Glutamatergic model psychoses: Prediction error, learning, and inference. *Neuropsychopharmacology.* doi:npp2010163 [pii] https://doi.org/10.1038/npp.2010.163

Corlett, P. R., Taylor, J. R., Wang, X. J., Fletcher, P. C., & Krystal, J. H. (2010). Toward a neurobiology of delusions. *Progress in Neurobiology, 92*(3), 345–369. https://doi.org/10.1016/j.pneurobio.2010.06.007

Corrigan, P. W. (2012). Research and the elimination of the stigma of mental illness. *The British Journal of Psychiatry, 201*(1), 7–8. https://doi.org/10.1192/bjp.bp.111.103382

Dalley, J. W., Laane, K., Theobald, D. E., Armstrong, H. C., Corlett, P. R., Chudasama, Y., & Robbins, T. W. (2005). Time-limited modulation of appetitive Pavlovian memory by D1 and NMDA receptors in the nucleus accumbens. *Proceedings of the National Academy of Sciences of the United States of America, 102*(17), 6189–6194. https://doi.org/10.1073/pnas.0502080102

Daw, N. D., Niv, Y., & Dayan, P. (2005). Uncertainty-based competition between prefrontal and dorsolateral striatal systems for behavioral control. *Nature Neuroscience, 8*(12), 1704–1711.

Dayan, P., Kakade, S., & Montague, P. R. (2000). Learning and selective attention. *Nature Neuroscience, 3*(Suppl), 1218–1223. https://doi.org/10.1038/81504

Dickinson, A. (2001). The 28th Bartlett memorial lecture causal learning: An associative analysis. *The Quarterly Journal of Experimental Psychology. B, 54*(1), 3–25.

Dima, D., Roiser, J. P., Dietrich, D. E., Bonnemann, C., Lanfermann, H., Emrich, H. M., & Dillo, W. (2009). Understanding why patients with schizophrenia do not perceive the hollow-mask illusion using dynamic causal modelling. *NeuroImage, 46*(4), 1180–1186. https://doi.org/10.1016/j.neuroimage.2009.03.033

Doll, B. B., Jacobs, W. J., Sanfey, A. G., & Frank, M. J. (2009). Instructional control of reinforcement learning: A behavioral and neurocomputational investigation. *Brain Research, 1299*, 74–94. https://doi.org/10.1016/j.brainres.2009.07.007

Doll, B. B., Waltz, J. A., Cockburn, J., Brown, J. K., Frank, M. J., & Gold, J. M. (2014, June). Reduced susceptibility to confirmation bias in schizophrenia. *Cognitive, Affective & Behavioral Neuroscience CABN, 14*(2), 715–728.

Ehrsson, H. H., Holmes, N. P., & Passingham, R. E. (2005). Touching a rubber hand: Feeling of body ownership is associated with activity in multisensory brain areas. *The Journal of Neuroscience, 25*(45), 10564–10573. https://doi.org/10.1523/JNEUROSCI.0800-05.2005

Fear, C. F., & Healy, D. (1997). Probabilistic reasoning in obsessive-compulsive and delusional disorders. *Psychological Medicine, 27*(1), 199–208.

Festinger, L. (1962). Cognitive dissonance. *Scientific American, 207*, 93–102.

Festinger, L., Riecken, H. W., & Schachter, S. (1956). *When prophecy fails*. Minneapolis: University of Minnesota.

Fineberg, S. K., Steinfeld, M., Brewer, J. A., & Corlett, P. R. (2014). A computational account of borderline personality disorder: Impaired predictive learning about self and others through bodily simulation. *Frontiers in Psychiatry, 5*, 111. https://doi.org/10.3389/fpsyt.2014.00111

Fleminger, S. (1992). Seeing is believing: The role of 'preconscious' perceptual processing in delusional misidentification. *The British Journal of Psychiatry, 160*, 293–303.

Fletcher, P. C., & Frith, C. D. (2009). Perceiving is believing: A Bayesian approach to explaining the positive symptoms of schizophrenia. *Nature Reviews Neuroscience, 10*(1), 48–58.

Fodor, J. A. (1975). *The language of thought*. New York: Crowell.

Fodor, J. A. (1983). *The modularity of mind: An essay on faculty psychology*. Cambridge, MA: MIT Press.

Fodor, J. A. (2000). *The mind Doesn't work that way*. Cambridge, MA: MIT.

Fotopoulou, A. (2014). Time to get rid of the 'Modular' in neuropsychology: A unified theory of anosognosia as aberrant predictive coding. *Journal of Neuropsychology, 8*(1), 1–19. https://doi.org/10.1111/jnp.12010

Frank, M. J., Moustafa, A. A., Haughey, H. M., Curran, T., & Hutchison, K. E. (2007). Genetic triple dissociation reveals multiple roles for dopamine in reinforcement learning. *Proceedings of the National Academy of Sciences of the United States of America, 104*(41), 16311–16316. https://doi.org/10.1073/pnas.0706111104

Friston, K., & Frith, C. (2015). A duet for one. *Consciousness and Cognition, 36*, 390–405. https://doi.org/10.1016/j.concog.2014.12.003

Friston, K., & Kiebel, S. (2009). Predictive coding under the free-energy principle. *Philosophical Transactions of the Royal Society of London. Series B, Biological Sciences, 364*(1521), 1211–1221. https://doi.org/10.1098/rstb.2008.0300

Friston, K., Sengupta, B., & Auletta, G. (2014). Cognitive dynamics: From attractors to active inference. *Proceedings of the Institute of Electronical and Electronics Engineers, 102*(4), 427–445. https://doi.org/10.1109/JPROC.2014.2306251

Friston, K. J., Daunizeau, J., Kilner, J., & Kiebel, S. J. (2010). Action and behavior: A free-energy formulation. *Biological Cybernetics, 102*(3), 227–260. https://doi.org/10.1007/s00422-010-0364-z

Garety, P. (1991). Reasoning and delusions. *The British Journal of Psychiatry, 14*(Supplement), 14–18.

Garety, P. A. (1992). Making sense of delusions. *Psychiatry, 55*(3), 282–291; discussion 292-286.

Garety, P. A., Hemsley, D. R., & Wessely, S. (1991). Reasoning in deluded schizophrenic and paranoid patients. Biases in performance on a probabilistic inference task. *Journal of Nervous and Mental Disease, 179*(4), 194–201.

Gibbs, A. A., & David, A. S. (2003). Delusion formation and insight in the context of affective disturbance. *Epidemiologia e Psichiatria Sociale, 12*(3), 167–174.

Gray, J. A. (1993). Consciousness, schizophrenia and scientific theory. *Ciba Foundation Symposium, 174*, 263–273 discussion 273-281.

Gray, J. A. (1998a). Abnormal contents of consciousness: The transition from automatic to controlled processing. *Advances in Neurology, 77*, 195–208; discussion 208-111.

Gray, J. A. (1998b). Integrating schizophrenia. *Schizophrenia Bulletin, 24*(2), 249–266.

Gray, J. A., Feldon, J., Rawlins, J. N. P., Hemsley, D., & Smith, A. D. (1991). The neuropsychology of schizophrenia. *The Behavioral and Brain Sciences, 14*, 1–84.

Greenwald, A. G. (1980). The totalitarian ego. *American Psychologist, 35*(7), 603–618.

Grossberg, S. (2000, July). How hallucinations may arise from brain mechanisms of learning, attention, and volition. *Journal of the International Neuropsychological Society : JINS, 6*(5), 583–592.

Halligan, P. W., & David, A. S. (2001). Cognitive neuropsychiatry: Towards a scientific psychopathology. *Nature Reviews. Neuroscience, 2*(3), 209–215.

Helmholtz, H. von. (1867). Handbuch der physiologischen Optik. Leipzig,: Voss.

Helmholtz, H. von. (1878/1971). The facts of perception. In R. Kahl (Ed.), *Selected Writings of Herman von Helmholtz*. Middletown, CT: Weslyan University Press.

Hemsley, D. R. (1993). A simple (or simplistic?) cognitive model for schizophrenia. *Behaviour Research and Therapy, 31*(7), 633–645.

Hemsley, D. R. (2005). The schizophrenic experience: Taken out of context? *Schizophrenia Bulletin, 31*(1), 43–53. https://doi.org/10.1093/schbul/sbi003

Hemsley, D. R., & Garety, P. A. (1986). The formation and maintenance of delusions: A Bayesian analysis. *The British Journal of Psychiatry, 149*, 51–56.
Heyes, C. (2010). Where do mirror neurons come from? *Neuroscience and Biobehavioral Reviews, 34*(4), 575–583. https://doi.org/10.1016/j.neubiorev.2009.11.007
Heyser, C. J., Fienberg, A. A., Greengard, P., & Gold, L. H. (2000). DARPP-32 knockout mice exhibit impaired reversal learning in a discriminated operant task. *Brain Research, 867*(1–2), 122–130.
Hickok, G. (2013). Do mirror neurons subserve action understanding? *Neuroscience Letters, 540*, 56–58. https://doi.org/10.1016/j.neulet.2012.11.001
Hirstein, W., & Ramachandran, V. S. (1997). Capgras syndrome: A novel probe for understanding the neural representation of the identity and familiarity of persons. *Proceedings of the Royal Society B: Biological Sciences, 264*(1380), 437–444.
Honsberger, M. J., Taylor, J. R., & Corlett, P. R. (2015). Memories reactivated under ketamine are subsequently stronger: A potential pre-clinical behavioral model of psychosis. *Schizophrenia Research*. https://doi.org/10.1016/j.schres.2015.02.009
Howes, O. D., Montgomery, A. J., Asselin, M. C., Murray, R. M., Valli, I., Tabraham, P., … Grasby, P. M. (2009). Elevated striatal dopamine function linked to prodromal signs of schizophrenia. *Archives of General Psychiatry, 66*(1), 13–20.
Hume, D. (1739/2007). *A treatise of human nature*. Oxford, UK: Oxford University Press.
Hume, D. (1900). *An enquiry concerning human understanding*. Chicago: The Open Court Publishing Co.; etc.
Huq, S. F., Garety, P. A., & Hemsley, D. R. (1988). Probabilistic judgements in deluded and non-deluded subjects. *The Quarterly Journal of Experimental Psychology, 40*(4), 801–812.
Johnson, D. D., & Fowler, J. H. (2011). The evolution of overconfidence. *Nature, 477*(7364), 317–320. https://doi.org/10.1038/nature10384
Johnson, M. K., & Raye, C. L. (1981). Reality monitoring. *Psychological Review, 88*(1), 67–85. https://doi.org/10.1037//0033-295x.88.1.67
Jones, S. R., & Fernyhough, C. (2007). Thought as action: Inner speech, self-monitoring, and auditory verbal hallucinations. *Consciousness and Cognition, 16*(2), 391–399. https://doi.org/10.1016/j.concog.2005.12.003
Kahneman, D. (2011). *Thinking, fast and slow*. New York: Farrar, Straus and Giroux.
Kahneman, D., Slovic, P., & Tversky, A. (1982). *Judgment under uncertainty*. Cambridge, UK: Cambridge University Press.
Kamin, L. (1969). Predictability, surprise, attention, and conditioning. In B. A. Campbell & R. M. Church (Eds.), *Punishment and aversive behavior*. New York: Appleton-Century-Crofts.

Kaney, S., & Bentall, R. P. (1992). Persecutory delusions and the self-serving bias. Evidence from a contingency judgment task. *The Journal of Nervous and Mental Disease, 180*(12), 773–780.

Kapur, S. (2003). Psychosis as a state of aberrant salience: A framework linking biology, phenomenology, and pharmacology in schizophrenia. *The American Journal of Psychiatry, 160*(1), 13–23.

Kapur, S. (2004). How antipsychotics become anti-"psychotic"—From dopamine to salience to psychosis. *Trends in Pharmacological Sciences, 25*(8), 402–406.

Kapur, S., Mizrahi, R., & Li, M. (2005). From dopamine to salience to psychosis-linking biology, pharmacology and phenomenology of psychosis. *Schizophrenia Research, 79*(1), 59–68.

Kihlstrom, J. F., & Hoyt, I. P. (1988). Hypnosis and the psychology of delusions. In T. F. Oltmanns & B. A. Maher (Eds.), *Delusional beliefs*. New York: Wiley.

Kilner, J., Friston, K., & Frith, C. (2007). Predictive coding: An account of the mirror neuron system. *Cognitive Processing, 8*(3), 159–166. https://doi.org/10.1007/s10339-007-0170-2

Körding, K. P., & Wolpert, D. M. (2004). Bayesian integration in sensorimotor learning. *Nature, 427*(6971), 244–247. https://doi.org/10.1038/nature02169

Koster-Hale, J., & Saxe, R. (2013). Theory of mind: A neural prediction problem. *Neuron, 79*, 836–848.

Laruelle, M., Abi-Dargham, A., Gil, R., Kegeles, L., & Innis, R. (1999). Increased dopamine transmission in schizophrenia: Relationship to illness phases. *Biological Psychiatry, 46*(1), 56–72.

Lavin, A., Nogueira, L., Lapish, C. C., Wightman, R. M., Phillips, P. E., & Seamans, J. K. (2005). Mesocortical dopamine neurons operate in distinct temporal domains using multimodal signaling. *The Journal of Neuroscience, 25*(20), 5013–5023.

Lawson, R. P., Friston, K. J., & Rees, G. (2015). A more precise look at context in autism. *Proceedings of the National Academy of Sciences of the United States of America, 112*(38), E5226. https://doi.org/10.1073/pnas.1514212112

Lawson, R. P., Rees, G., & Friston, K. J. (2014). An aberrant precision account of autism. *Frontiers in Human Neuroscience, 8*, 302. https://doi.org/10.3389/fnhum.2014.00302

Lee, S. W., O'Doherty, J. P., & Shimojo, S. (2015). Neural computations mediating one-shot learning in the human brain. *PLoS Biology, 13*(4), e1002137. https://doi.org/10.1371/journal.pbio.1002137

Leff, J., Williams, G., Huckvale, M. A., Arbuthnot, M., & Leff, A. P. (2013). Computer-assisted therapy for medication-resistant auditory hallucinations: Proof-of-concept study. *The British Journal of Psychiatry: The Journal of Mental Science, 202*, 428–433. https://doi.org/10.1192/bjp.bp.112.124883

Locke, J. (1690/1976). *An essay concerning human unerstanding*. London: Dent.

Lord, C. G., Ross, L., & Lepper, M. R. (1979). Biased assimilation and attitude polarization: The effects of prior theories on subsequently considered evidence. *Journal of Personality and Social Psychology, 37*(11), 2098–2109.

Lupyan, G., & Clark, A. (2015). Words and the world: Predictive coding and the language-perception-cognition Interface. *Current Directions in Psychological Science, 24*(4), 279–284. https://doi.org/10.1177/0963721415570732

Mackintosh, N. J. (1975). A theory of attention: Variations in the associability of stimuli with reinforcement. *Psychological Review, 82*, 276–298.

Maher, B. A. (1974). Delusional thinking and perceptual disorder. *Journal of Individual Psychology, 30*(1), 98–113.

Maher, B. A. (1988a). Anomalous experience and delusional thinking: The logic of explanations. In T. F. Oltmanns & B. A. Maher (Eds.), *Delusional Beliefs* (pp. 15–33). New York: Wiley.

Maher, B. A. (1988b). *Delusions as normal theories*. New York: Wiley.

Marshall, L., Mathys, C., Ruge, D., de Berker, A. O., Dayan, P., Stephan, K. E., & Bestmann, S. (2016). Pharmacological fingerprints of contextual uncertainty. *PLoS Biology, 14*(11), e1002575. https://doi.org/10.1371/journal.pbio.1002575

McKay, R., Langdon, R., & Coltheart, M. (2005). "Sleights of mind": Delusions, defences, and self-deception. *Cognitive Neuropsychiatry, 10*(4), 305–326.

McKay, R., Langdon, R., & Coltheart, M. (2006). Need for closure, jumping to conclusions, and decisiveness in delusion-prone individual. *Journal of Nervous and Mental Disease, 194*(6), 422–426.

McKay, R. T., & Dennett, D. C. (2009). The evolution of misbelief. *The Behavioral and Brain Sciences, 32*(6), 493–510; discussion 510-461. https://doi.org/10.1017/S0140525X09990975.

McLaren, I. P., & Dickinson, A. (1990). The conditioning connection. *Philosophical Transactions of the Royal Society of London. Series B, Biological Sciences, 329*(1253), 179–186. https://doi.org/10.1098/rstb.1990.0163

Mendoza, P. (1978). [In memoriam of Gerardo Varela). *Gaceta medica de Mexico, 114*(5), 250.

Menon, M., Pomarol-Clotet, E., McKenna, P. J., & McCarthy, R. A. (2006). Probabilistic reasoning in schizophrenia: A comparison of the performance of deluded and nondeluded schizophrenic patients and exploration of possible cognitive underpinnings. *Cognitive Neuropsychiatry, 11*(6), 521–536. https://doi.org/10.1080/13546800544000046

Menon, M., Anderson, A., Schmitz, T., Graff, A., Korostil, M., Mamo, D., et al. (2011). Exploring the neural correlates of delusions of reference: An fMRI study. *Biological Psychiatry, 70*(12), 1127–1133.

Meyer-Lindenberg, A., Straub, R. E., Lipska, B. K., Verchinski, B. A., Goldberg, T., Callicott, J. H., … Weinberger, D. R. (2007). Genetic evidence implicating DARPP-32 in human frontostriatal structure, function, and cognition. *The Journal of Clinical Investigation, 117*(3), 672–682.

Michotte, A. (1963). *The perception of causality*. Oxford, England: Basic Books.

Miller, R. (1976). Schizophrenic psychology, associative learning and the role of forebrain dopamine. *Medical Hypotheses, 2*(5), 203–211.

Miller, R. (1993). Striatal dopamine in reward and attention: A system for understanding the symptomatology of acute schizophrenia and mania. *International Review of Neurobiology, 35*, 161–278.

Moran, P. M., Al-Uzri, M. M., Watson, J., & Reveley, M. A. (2003). Reduced Kamin blocking in non paranoid schizophrenia: Associations with schizotypy. *Journal of Psychiatric Research, 37*(2), 155–163.

Morgan, H. L., Turner, D. C., Corlett, P. R., Absalom, A. R., Adapa, R., Arana, F. S., … Fletcher, P. C. (2011). Exploring the impact of ketamine on the experience of illusory body ownership. *Biological Psychiatry, 69*(1), 35–41. https://doi.org/10.1016/j.biopsych.2010.07.032

Moritz, S., & Woodward, T. S. (2005). Jumping to conclusions in delusional and non-delusional schizophrenic patients. *The British Journal of Clinical Psychology/The British Psychological Society, 44*.(Pt 2, 193–207. https://doi.org/10.1348/014466505X35678

Moutoussis, M., Bentall, R. P., El-Deredy, W., & Dayan, P. (2011). Bayesian modelling of Jumping-to-Conclusions bias in delusional patients. *Cognitive Neuropsychiatry, 16*(5), 422–447. https://doi.org/10.1080/13546805.2010.548678

Nickerson, R. S. (1998). Confirmation bias: A ubiquitous phenomenon in many guises. *Review of General Psychology, 2*(2), 175–220.

Nyhan, B., & Reifler, J. (2013). *Which corrections work?* Washington, DC: New America Foundation.

O'Tuathaigh, C. M., Salum, C., Young, A. M., Pickering, A. D., Joseph, M. H., & Moran, P. M. (2003). The effect of amphetamine on Kamin blocking and overshadowing. *Behavioural Pharmacology, 14*(4), 315–322. https://doi.org/10.1097/01.fbp.0000080416.18561.3e

Palmer, C. J., Seth, A. K., & Hohwy, J. (2015). The felt presence of other minds: Predictive processing, counterfactual predictions, and mentalising in autism. *Consciousness and Cognition, 36*, 376–389. https://doi.org/10.1016/j.concog.2015.04.007

Pavlov, I. P. (1927). *Conditioned reflexes: An investigation of the physiological activity of the cerebral cortex* (G. V. Anrep, Trans.). New York: Dover Publications.

Pearce, J. M., & Hall, G. (1980). A model for Pavlovian learning: Variations in the effectiveness of conditioned but not of unconditioned stimuli. *Psychological Review, 87*(6), 532–552. https://doi.org/10.1037/0033-295x.87.6.532

Pearl, J. (1988). *Probabilistic Reasoning in Intelligent Systems* (Revised second printing ed.). San Mateo, CA: Morgan Kaufmann Publishers Inc.

Pearl, J., & Russel, S. (2001). Bayesian networks. In M. Arbib (Ed.), *Handbook of brain theory and neural networks*. Cambridge, MA: MIT Press.

Peirce. (1931–58). *Collected papers of Charles Sanders Peirce* (Vol. 1–6). Cambridge, MA: Harvard University Press.

Peled, A., Pressman, A., Geva, A. B., & Modai, I. (2003). Somatosensory evoked potentials during a rubber-hand illusion in schizophrenia. *Schizophrenia Research, 64*(2–3), 157–163.

Pessiglione, M., Petrovic, P., Daunizeau, J., Palminteri, S., Dolan, R. J., & Frith, C. D. (2008). Subliminal instrumental conditioning demonstrated in the human brain. *Neuron, 59*(4), 561–567. https://doi.org/10.1016/j.neuron.2008.07.005

Plato. (350 B.C./1999). *Phaedo* (D. Gallop, Trans.). Oxford, UK: Oxford University Press.

Pomarol-Clotet, E., Honey, G. D., Murray, G. K., Corlett, P. R., Absalom, A. R., Lee, M., … Fletcher, P. C. (2006). Psychological effects of ketamine in healthy volunteers. Phenomenological study. *The British Journal of Psychiatry, 189*, 173–179.

Powers, A. R., Mathys, C., & Corlett, P. R. (2017). Pavlovian conditioning-induced hallucinations result from overweighting of perceptual priors. *Science, 357*(6351), 596–600. https://doi.org/10.1126/science.aan3458

Powers, A. R., III, Kelley, M., & Corlett, P. R. (2016). Hallucinations as top-down effects on perception. *Biological Psychiatry: CNNI, 1*, 393–400.

Proulx, T., Inzlicht, M., & Harmon-Jones, E. (2012). Understanding all inconsistency compensation as a palliative response to violated expectations. *Trends in Cognitive Science, 16*(5), 285–291. https://doi.org/10.1016/j.tics.2012.04.002

Quine, W. V., & Quine, W. V. (1951). Two dogmas of empiricism. *Philosophical Review, 60*, 20–43.

Rescorla, R. A., & Wagner, A. R. (1972). A theory of Pavlovian conditioning: Variations in the effectiveness of reinforcement and non-reinforcement. In A. H. Black & W. F. Prokasy (Eds.), *Classical conditioning II: Current research and theory* (pp. 64–99). New York: Appleton-Century-Crofts.

Robbins, T. W., & Everitt, B. J. (1996). Neurobehavioural mechanisms of reward and motivation. *Current Opinion in Neurobiology, 6*(2), 228–236.

Robinson, T. E., & Berridge, K. C. (2001). Incentive-sensitization and addiction. *Addiction, 96*(1), 103–114.

Schneider, K. (1957, September). Primary & secondary symptoms in schizophrenia. *Fortschritte der Neurologie, Psychiatrie, und ihrer Grenzgebiete, 25*(9), 487–490.

Seth, A. K. (2013). Interoceptive inference, emotion, and the embodied self. *Trends in Cognitive Sciences, 17*(11), 565–573. https://doi.org/10.1016/j.tics.2013.09.007

Seth, A. K., Suzuki, K., & Critchley, H. D. (2011). An interoceptive predictive coding model of conscious presence. *Frontiers in Psychology, 2*, 395. https://doi.org/10.3389/fpsyg.2011.00395

Shanks, D. R., & Channon, S. (2002). Effects of a secondary task on "implicit" sequence learning: Learning or performance? *Psychological Research, 66*(2), 99–109.

Snyder, M., & Swann, W. B., Jr. (1978). Behavioural confirmation in social interaction; from social perception to social reality. *Journal of Experimental Social Psychology, 14*, 148–162.

Steinberg, E. E., Keiflin, R., Boivin, J. R., Witten, I. B., Deisseroth, K., & Janak, P. H. (2013). A causal link between prediction errors, dopamine neurons and learning. *Nature Neuroscience, 16*(7), 966–973. https://doi.org/10.1038/nn.3413

Stephan, K. E., Friston, K. J., & Frith, C. D. (2009). Dysconnection in schizophrenia: From abnormal synaptic plasticity to failures of self-monitoring. *Schizophrenia Bulletin, 35*(3), 509–527. https://doi.org/10.1093/schbul/sbn176

Svenningsson, P., Tzavara, E. T., Carruthers, R., Rachleff, I., Wattler, S., Nehls, M., ... Greengard, P. (2003). Diverse psychotomimetics act through a common signaling pathway. *Science, 302*(5649), 1412–1415.

Tang, J., Morgan, H. L., Liao, Y., Corlett, P. R., Wang, D., Li, H., ... Chen, X. (2015). Chronic administration of ketamine mimics the perturbed sense of body ownership associated with schizophrenia. *Psychopharmacology, 232*(9), 1515–1526. https://doi.org/10.1007/s00213-014-3782-0

Taylor, S. E., & Fiske, S. T. (1978). *Salience, attention and attribution: Top of the head phenomena* (Vol. 11). San Diego, CA: Academic.

Teufel, C., Naresh, S., Veronika, D., Jesus, P., Johanna, F., Puja, R. M., ... Paul, C. F. (2015). Shift toward prior knowledge confers a perceptual advantage in early psychosis and psychosis-prone healthy individuals. *Proceedings of the National Academy of Sciences, 112*(43), 13401–13406. https://doi.org/10.1073/pnas.1503916112

Tranel, D., & Damasio, A. R. (1985). Knowledge without awareness: An autonomic index of facial recognition by prosopagnosics. *Science, 228*(4706), 1453–1454.

Varela, F. G. (1971). Self-consciousness: Adaptation or epiphenomenon? *Studium generale; Zeitschrift fur die Einheit der Wissenschaften im Zusammenhang ihrer Begriffsbildungen und Forschungsmethoden, 24*(4), 426–439.

Wada, M., Takano, K., Ora, H., Ide, M., & Kansaku, K. (2016). The rubber tail illusion as evidence of body ownership in mice. *The Journal of Neuroscience, 36*(43), 11133–11137. https://doi.org/10.1523/JNEUROSCI.3006-15.2016

Warren, H. C. (1921). *A history of the association psychology*. New York: Charles Scribner's Sons.

Widrow, B., & Hoff, M. E., Jr. (1960). *Adaptive switching circuits*. Paper presented at the IRE WESCON convention rec.

Yau, J. O., & McNally, G. P. (2015). Pharmacogenetic excitation of dorsomedial prefrontal cortex restores fear prediction error. *The Journal of Neuroscience, 35*(1), 74–83. https://doi.org/10.1523/JNEUROSCI.3777-14.2015

Young, G. (2008). Capgras delusion: An interactionist model. *Consciousness and Cognition, 17*(3), 863–876.

Zmigrod, L., Garrison, J. R., Carr, J., & Simons, J. S. (2016). The neural mechanisms of hallucinations: A quantitative meta-analysis of neuroimaging studies. *Neuroscience and Biobehavioral Reviews, 69*, 113–123. https://doi.org/10.1016/j.neubiorev.2016.05.037

CHAPTER 3

Delusions and Other Beliefs

Richard P. Bentall

Abstract The difficulty of distinguishing between delusions and non-pathological beliefs has taxed some of the greatest minds in psychiatry. This chapter argues that this question cannot be resolved without first having an understanding of what is involved in holding an ordinary belief. Although we should not assume that ordinary-language words such as 'belief' will correspond with a specific psychological mechanism or process, sufficient evidence is available from diverse areas of psychology to reach some conclusions about what happens when someone 'believes' something. Beliefs are propositions about the world that are generated dynamically, often during interactions with other people, and therefore depend on the human capacity for language. Although many beliefs are mundane, it is possible to identify a class of master interpretive systems that includes political ideologies and religious belief systems, which are highly resistant to challenge and capable of generating considerable emotion. These systems seem to depend not only on the ability to generate propositions about the world but also on implicit cognitive processes that are related to fundamental biological and social needs, for example the need to avoid contagion, the need to form close intimate relationships or

R. P. Bentall (✉)
Clinical Psychology Unit, Department of Psychology, University of Sheffield, Sheffield, UK
e-mail: r.bentall@sheffield.ac.uk

L. Bortolotti (ed.), *Delusions in Context*,
https://doi.org/10.1007/978-3-319-97202-2_3

the need to avoid out-groups. Delusions share many of the properties of master interpretive systems but differ because they are idiosyncratic. They may arise when individuals are very isolated or if they lack the cognitive tools to function effectively in groups. Further progress in understanding delusions is likely to be made if research is informed by findings from political psychology and the psychology of religion.

Keywords Delusion • Belief • Belief systems • Political ideologies • Master interpretive systems • Psychology of religion • Political psychology

3.1 Introduction

Delusions, described in the latest edition of the American Psychiatric Association's (2013) diagnostic manual as, "fixed beliefs that are not amenable to change in light of conflicting evidence", are a commonly recorded symptom of severe mental illness, observed in patients with a wide range of diagnoses including schizophrenia, schizoaffective disorder, bipolar disorder and major depression. In recent years, paranoid (persecutory) beliefs in particular have been the subject of extensive psychological investigation, leading to well-developed psychological models and a rich experimental literature (Bentall, Corcoran, Howard, Blackwood, & Kinderman, 2001; Freeman, 2016). However, both standard psychiatric accounts and psychological approaches have treated delusions as *sui generis*. At the same time, within the philosophical literature, there has been a vigorous debate about the doxastic nature of delusions – whether they can be said to be beliefs at all (Bortolotti, 2018).

Arguably, these developments reflect lack of clarity about the concept of belief. It is difficult to overstate how widely this concept is employed in clinical psychology (e.g. in cognitive models of depression; Beck, 1987), social psychology (e.g. models of social reasoning such as attribution theory; Weiner, 2008), and cognitive science (e.g. models of semantic knowledge; Martin, 2009). Within the social sciences such as sociology, political science, anthropology and history, the concept is so ubiquitous that documenting its usage would be a near-impossible task. Indeed, some philosophers have attempted to draw a distinction between the human and natural sciences on the grounds that human behaviour is rule-governed, determined by reasons and hence (implicitly at least) belief-driven (Winch, 1958).

In this essay, I will argue that, despite the absence of an over-arching theory of what is involved when someone believes something, sufficient evidence can be gleaned from diverse areas of psychology to reach some important conclusions and, furthermore, that these conclusions illuminate both similarities and differences between the delusions of psychiatric patients and the beliefs of ordinary people. The spirit behind this analysis, which is contrary to the standard psychiatric approach, involves starting with the assumption that delusional and non-delusional beliefs are similar phenomena until proven otherwise.

3.2 Delusions

Throughout the history of psychiatry the assumption that delusions and ordinary beliefs and attitudes are different has been coupled with the recognition that it is difficult to state exactly where the difference lies. This difficulty has practical implications, particularly for psychiatric diagnosticians and in legal contexts when efforts are made to determine the culpability of people who commit serious crimes. The cases of Ron and Dan Lafferty in the United States (Krakauer, 2003) and Anders Breivik in Norway (Melle, 2013) illustrate this problem. The Lafferty brothers, devout Mormon fundamentalists, were convicted of murdering their sister in law and her infant daughter in 1983, apparently at the instigation of messages received from Jesus Christ; one of the brothers later proclaimed himself to be the prophet Elijah. Breivik committed a bombing and a mass shooting in Norway in 2011, killing seventy-seven mostly young people, apparently believing himself to be a member of a mysterious group, the Knight Templars, defending Europe against Islamist influences. In both cases, there was extensive debate amongst mental health professionals about whether the beliefs motivating the crimes could be said to be delusional and therefore evidence of mental illness. Although, in both cases, juries ultimately decided that the perpetrators were culpable for their crimes, it was striking that mental health professionals continued to be divided on the issue even after convictions had been obtained.

Phenomenological data has often been appealed to when attempting to distinguish between delusional and non-delusional beliefs and, indeed, the failure of mental health professionals to reach a definitive position on the Breivik case has been attributed to the failure to attend to this kind of evidence (Parnas, 2013). In his celebrated analysis of the problem, Karl Jaspers (1913/1963) noted that delusional beliefs seemed bizarre to others, are firmly held and are resistant to counter argument. However, he held that true delusions are distinguishable from 'delusional-like ideas' because they often occur suddenly and are "ununderstandable" in the sense that they cannot be understood in terms of the individual's background experiences and personality. Later phenomenologists, such as Conrad, argued that delusions are the consequence of subtle changes in the way that the individual experiences the self and the world, and can therefore be identified by the emotional and perceptual changes that often preceded the development of the belief (Bovet & Parnas, 1993), a position which is said to be supported by detailed analysis of patients' experiences (Parnas, Handest, Jansson, & Sæbye, 2005). A further observation that is said to call the doxastic nature of delusions into question is 'double book keeping' – the failure of patients to act in ways that are consistent with their delusional statements (Sass, 2014), a phenomenon that is said to show lack of normal commitment to beliefs, and which appears to place the patient in a position akin to solipsism (Sass, 1994). Notice that, in these analyses, a common sense concept of 'belief' is typically unanalysed and taken for granted.

It is possible to question the project to phenomenologically deconstruct delusions on philosophical grounds. The phenomenological approach places great emphasis on patient's ability to describe private experiences and yet, as the later Wittgenstein, (1953) and sophisticated 'radical' behaviourists have pointed out (Skinner, 1945), reporting private events is a quite different type of activity to the reporting of public experiences. This is because, during ontogeny, the acquisition of words to describe events requires that both the perceiver and others have access to the events in question (I can be taught by someone else to accurately name a "table" or corrected if I mistake it for a "chair"), a condition which is absent when talking about the inner world available to only one observer. Indeed, when examining historically important examples of delusional self-reports, notably the celebrated case of Daniel Schreber (1903/1955), the struggle to describe such experiences is palpable.

Empirical studies provide further grounds for questioning the criteria for delusions represented in both classification manuals and the phenomenological literature. First, delusions may be held less rigidly than often supposed, and conviction in them may be no greater than for other idiosyncratic or religious beliefs and attitudes (Brett-Jones, Garety, & Hemsley, 1987; Colbert, Peters, & Garety, 2010). Conversely, other kinds of beliefs, notoriously political beliefs, are often held very rigidly (Taber & Lodge,

2013), or shift in ways that seem to have very little to do with the rational appraisal of evidence (Achen & Bartels, 2016). Second, psychometric studies show that, in the case of paranoid beliefs in particular, the delusions of psychiatric patients exist on a continuum with less severe analogues experienced in everyday life (Bebbington et al., 2013; Elahi, Perez Algorta, Varese, McIntyre, & Bentall, 2017). Third, research with psychiatric patients and epidemiological samples has shown that abnormal beliefs are often preceded by life events that can be meaningfully linked to the beliefs. For example, paranoid beliefs are often preceded by severe disruptions of early attachment relationships (Bentall, Wickham, Shevlin, & Varese, 2012; Sitko, Bentall, Shevlin, O'Sullivan, & Sellwood, 2014) and/or experiences of victimization (Janssen et al., 2003). It has also been pointed out that the phenomenon of double book-keeping may be much less ubiquitous in the lives of psychiatric patients than has sometimes been thought (so far as I am aware, no commentator on the Breivik case disputed his delusional status on the grounds that he actually killed people) and can possibly be accounted for by supposing that the deluded person lacks the motivation to act on their beliefs (Bortolotti & Broome, 2012). Finally, anomalous perceptual experiences are often reported before the onset of at least one kind of belief that is widely accepted to be non-delusional, namely religious belief (Hardy, 1979).

Of course, none of these observations rule out the possibility that some of the beliefs expressed by psychiatric patients are qualitatively different from those of ordinary people. However, to see whether this is the case, we surely need to have some conception of what is involved when ordinary people express a belief.

3.3 What Are Beliefs? The Inner List Idea

If the concept of delusion is slippery, the same is undoubtedly true of the concept of belief. A modern attempt to define the concept can be found in the *Stanford Encyclopedia of Philosophy* (Schwitzgebel, 2015):

> Contemporary analytic philosophers of mind generally use the term 'belief' to refer to the attitude we have, roughly, whenever we take something to be the case or regard it as true. To believe something, in this sense, need not involve actively reflecting on it: Of the vast number of things ordinary adults believe, only a few can be at the fore of the mind at any single time.... Many of the things we believe, in the relevant sense, are quite mundane: that we

have heads, that it's the 21st century, that a coffee mug is on the desk. Forming beliefs is thus one of the most basic and important features of the mind.

When attempting to make sense of beliefs from a psychological perspective, it is important to acknowledge that everyday language may provide a poor taxonomy of human mental processes. Indeed, the English language provides many other concepts that appear to overlap with the concept of 'belief' to some degree, for example 'attitude' (the cognitive component of which can be thought of as, roughly, a belief about the value of something), and 'prediction' (roughly, a belief about what will happen in the future).

Some radical critics of folk psychology (the kind of psychological concepts we employ in everyday life), for example eliminative philosophers such as Churchland (1986) and Stich (1996), have argued that we have no warrant to believe that folk psychological concepts such as belief will correspond with discoverable psychological or neural processes at all, and that they therefore should be dispensed with in any scientific account of human behaviour. However, the fact that I have felt compelled to use the word 'belief' to describe their position illustrates, I think, its fatal flaw.

I will therefore take the more pragmatic approach of identifying those mechanisms that seem to be involved when people behave in ways that we would describe as 'believing'. (Much of what I will say will also apply to what human beings do when they are said to have an attitude towards something, or to predict something.) Before proceeding, however, it will first be useful to dispense with a common misconception about beliefs which, I think, lies behind the objections made by eliminativists (who, on looking in the brain see nothing that seems to correspond to the concept of 'belief') and certain types of methodological behaviourists (for example, Watson, 1924) who object to talking about private psychological phenomena on the grounds that they are unobservable.

The earliest references to belief in the English language all occur within a theological context. For example, the Oxford English Dictionary attributes the first recorded use of the mental conviction form of 'belief' as the Middle English "Ðesne laf we æteð þonne we mid bileafan gað to halige husle ure hælendes lichame" ("This bread we eat when we with faith go to the holy Eucharist of Our Lord's body"), which appears in Ælfric's Homily on Nativity of Christ, written in about 1175. Of course, it is entirely possible that this early association between belief and religion simply reflects the fact that nearly all of the earliest English-language texts were written by monks, but it is more likely because the creation of theological doctrine implies the need for a list-like approach in which beliefs can be codified and decisions can be made about who is a true believer and who is not. Indeed, in the face of competition between different Christian cults in the first millennium, the necessity arose to make people accountable for their beliefs, and so the early Church devoted considerable energy towards the development of checklists of beliefs, known as *creeds* (MacCulloch, 2009).

Speculating somewhat, the invention of creeds was perhaps the cultural origin a pervasive conception of beliefs as a kind of inner list that can be read out when an individual is interrogated (and which the individual may decide not to report accurately, in which case he or she is said to lie). It is not difficult to see why the inner list conception is problematic. We are capable of believing some things completely de novo (I believe that there are no convenience stores on the far side of Jupiter but I have never had this thought before today). Just as importantly, during everyday conversations, especially arguments and debates, what we assert to be the case (what we believe) may evolve as a conversation progresses; indeed, in many cases the establishment of what is factually the case occurs socially, through interactions with other people (Edwards & Potter, 1992). This kind of online elaboration, in which claims about what is the case are constructed and defended using various rhetorical strategies, so that what is true might be said to be negotiated, is not only observed during political debates and family arguments but also when psychiatric patients are challenged (Georgaca, 2000) and has a number of important implications.

The most important theoretical implication is that we should think of believing as a kind of activity or behaviour that evolves over time. Believing is something that we do, and therefore more like a performance than a script. Because believing is a dynamic process, there can be no final account of what we believe. To borrow a metaphor from Dennett (1991) our beliefs therefore appear as an endless series of multiple drafts, each one to be replaced by a further draft. Rather than thinking about beliefs (noun) we would better think about believing (verb).

A practical implication is that we should recognise that the way that believing is performed will vary according to circumstances, and that the spontaneous statement of a belief may involve very different processes to those involved in assenting to a belief presented by someone else. For this reason, simple questionnaire measures of beliefs have important limitations. As a researcher who has used measures of this kind in numerous studies, I hesitate to say that they have no value – clearly they do – but, when a person fills in a questionnaire, what they are really doing is stating how much they would be likely to agree with the beliefs of the questionnaire designer, which is quite a different thing to actually generating a belief. (Recent – at the time of writing in early 2018 – research on the British public's attitude towards leaving the European Union illustrates this point quite well. Whereas polling data seems to suggest that those who voted to leave have hardly changed their minds, focus groups in which people are encouraged to freely express their thoughts have revealed a substantial group of 'leavers' who, despite stating that they would probably vote to leave the EU again in the event of a second referendum, have serious doubts about the wisdom of doing so; Gaston, 2018).

3.4 Do Dogs Believe?

With the above caveats in mind, we can now move on to consider what kind of psychological mechanisms are involved when a person is said to believe something. A helpful starting point is to consider whether animals believe. It is self-evidently true that the reader's dog is unlikely to become a jihadi, but he will come downstairs at the appropriate time, stand in front of the cupboard containing his food and wag his tail hopefully. Can the dog be said to believe that the food is in the cabinet?

A rich tradition of empirical research, beginning in the behaviourist era but extending to the present day, has explored the intellectual capabilities of animals by investigating their ability to learn in various experimental situations. Much of this research has focused on either Pavlovian conditioning in which the animal learns associations between previously unrelated stimuli (for example, that a bell signals the arrival of food) or operant conditioning in which the animal learns that certain responses are associated with rewarding or unrewarding consequences (for example, that pressing a lever is followed by the delivery of food). Interestingly, when nonhuman vertebrate species are tested appropriately, it is difficult to discern substantial differences between them – goldfish can be trained to perform tricks of surprising complexity if rewarded; it is just difficult to find ways of rewarding goldfish (McPhail, 1982).

There has been a decades long debate about whether the full complexity of non-human mammalian behaviour can be accounted for by associative mechanisms (Pearce, 2008). It is important to note that these mechanisms are capable of not only associating but also evaluating (when a neutral stimulus is paired with a valued stimulus, the neutral stimulus acquires value) and anticipating (animals can use learned relationships between stimuli to predict future events). This latter property reveals that the associative system is much more sophisticated than was thought during the early days of behaviourism. In a celebrated series of studies, Wagner and Rescorla (1972) showed that mere contiguity between stimuli is insufficient for conditioning to occur; stimuli are only attended to by animals if they carry information about other important events in their environment. Hence, associative learning is a process that allows animals to predict the occurrence of evolutionarily salient events such as food or predators, and to select actions that either increase or decrease the likelihood of encountering those events. If this ability were considered sufficient to make an attribution of belief, then it would be reasonable to say that the dog believes that food is in the cupboard.

The ability that unambiguously separates human beings from other animal species is, of course, language. Many design features distinguish language from naturally-occurring animal communication systems (Hockett, 1959), but two particularly important ones are worth noting. First, the use of arbitrary symbols – words – allows human beings to talk about events that are not actually present ("black holes") and with a high level of abstraction ("democracy"). Second, the structure of language allows these words to be combined according to syntactic rules, facilitating the construction of propositions that incorporate complex conditional relations (for example, if-then rules as in, "If I don't complete this chapter soon, Lisa will be very unhappy"). This latter feature is hard to account for in terms of associative processes. Four decades-worth of attempts to teach symbol manipulation and language-related skills to non-human animals have produced largely negative or at best inconclusive results (Lyn, 2012; Pepperberg, 2017). In particular, syntax appears to be denied to non-human species (Terrace, Petitto, Sanders, & Bever, 1979; Yang, 2013). Certainly, outside the confines of narrow experimental procedures conducted within the animal laboratory, human being are the only species that spontaneously communicates with propositions, leading some to suggest that we occupy a kingdom of our own within the taxonomic structure of the natural world (Wolfe, 2016).

Although the human ability to construct verbal propositions has clearly played a crucial role in facilitating the development of science and culture, language is not merely a vehicle for transmitting complex ideas between individuals and across generations. When we communicate with ourselves, propositions provide a powerful tool for thinking. This idea was first developed by Pavlov (1941), who distinguished between what he termed the first signalling system (neural representation of the world) and the second signalling system ("speech ... being the signal of the first signals"). In a passage that seems to have prescient relevance for the present discussion, he cautioned that:

> On the one hand, numerous speech stimulations have removed us from reality, and we must always remember this in order not to distort our attitude to reality.... on the other hand, it is precisely speech which has made us human.

This idea was later turned into a developmental model by the Russian psychologist Lev Vygotsky (1962) whose seminal work, conducted in the 1930s, only became known in the English-speaking world decades after his death. Vygotsky argued that, during early child development, social speech is acquired first, and noted a stage between about two and four years of age when children speak out loud even if no one appears to be listening, a phenomenon he termed private speech. Piaget (1926) had labelled the same phenomenon egocentric speech because he believed it was the consequence of the child's failure to appreciate the absence of other people. Vygotsky's view, which is now widely accepted by child psychologists, was that private speech has a self-regulatory function and is addressed to the self. Private speech disappears later in development because it becomes internalized and silent, a phenomenon Vygotsky termed inner speech. There is not sufficient space here to detail more recent research on the role of language in thinking; suffice it to say that the ability to speak can fairly be described as a cognitive turbocharger that transforms human reasoning capacities and places us in a separate class to other species (see Fernyhough, 2016).

There has been some debate in the human experimental psychology literature about whether humans retain the associative system that governs animal behaviour. Although it seems unlikely that evolution would abandon a set of mechanisms that have proved so adaptive over millions of years, some experimental psychologists have argued that it is near impossible to demonstrate animal-like conditioning in human adults and, therefore, that human reasoning is entirely propositional (Brewer, 1974; Mitchell, de Houwer, & Lovibond, 2009). A problem faced when attempting conditioning studies with human adults is that it is very difficult to contrive experiments in which the participants cannot readily construct accurate propositional descriptions of the experimental setup. Hence, the research findings probably demonstrate the dominance of the propositional over the associative system when the relationships between stimuli are obvious. In other kinds of experiments (for example, when people attempt to learn complex rules about the permissible order of stimuli) associative learning appears to be more efficient (Reber, 1989).

In fact, over the past two decades a large volume of evidence from many strands of psychological research have suggested that human adults possess two learning mechanisms – one fast, intuitive, associative and shared with animals, the other slow, deliberative and propositional – leading to numerous proposals for two process accounts of human cognition (e.g. Evans, 2008; Gawronski & Bodenhausen, 2006; Kahneman, 2012). When the associative system is dominant, we react in ways that seem automatic and 'from the gut', in which case our responses are said to be implicit. As we will see shortly, implicit processes appear to play an important role in some kinds of human belief systems.

An important feature of propositions is that they can be assigned truth-values. The *Stanford Encyclopedia of Philosophy* definition of belief given earlier implies that this is also a key feature of human beliefs – if we believe X we not only state X but also have the attitude that X is true. In fact, the English language (and I am sure all other languages) allows us to calibrate the likely accuracy of our assertions with a considerable degree of sophistication ("I think that", "I expect that," "I hope that", "I am sure that", etc.). The psychological processes that allow us to calibrate our certainty when making statements about the world are not fully understood and well beyond the scope of this chapter, but obviously depend on a second order ability to reflect on the statements that we make. This ability falls within the general category of meta-representation, a process that appears to be restricted to the human species and which is undoubtedly closely linked to language, although the exact relationship continues to be a subject of lively debate (Sperber, 2000).

Crucially, the capacity for metarepresentation allows us not only to calibrate the certainty of our statements but also to designate beliefs as *our* beliefs – propositions that we take ownership of. Later, we will see that this concept of ownership probably helps to explain our resistance to changing our beliefs in the face of evidence that contradicts them. It also creates the opportunity for people to make judgments about what kinds of beliefs they should have, and to actively seek to cultivate particular beliefs. For example, an anthropological study of fundamentalist Christians in the southern states of America found that converts often did not describe themselves as believers but as people who were seeking to believe, so that the acquisition of true religious belief was seen as the culmination of a long period of effort and learning (Luhrmann, 2012).

However well established the association between the cupboard door and food may be, it seems doubtful to me that a dog, as it waits to be fed, can be said to be asserting the truth of the statement that the food is in the cupboard. The dog certainly cannot express nuanced judgments about the likelihood of the cupboard-food association being true, nor assert a claim of ownership over the expectation that the food is in the cupboard. For this reason, I think it is reasonable to say that a dog cannot believe, at least in the full sense that a human being can believe.

3.5 Master Interpretive Systems

The Stanford Encyclopedia definition quoted earlier notes that many beliefs are quite mundane (the examples given are that "it is the 21st century" or that "there is a coffee cup on my desk"). However, it is equally obvious that some of the things we believe are far from mundane and are in fact loaded with significance. When understanding whether there is anything unique about the delusions of psychiatric patients, the appropriate comparison may be these more emotionally salient beliefs, and in particular a class of belief phenomena that I will term master interpretive systems: *systems* because they involve not just one proposition but an organized system of generating propositions; *interpretive* because they reflect particular stances when interpreting the world; *master* because they tend to dominate all other ways in which human beings interpret the social world.

This type of belief system, which includes religious and political beliefs, is not limited to particular propositions although it includes them ("God created the world in seven days"; "Everywhere workers are exploited by the ruling class"). Rather, master interpretive systems should be thought of as clusters or networks of inter-related propositions that address multiple facets of human life and the dilemmas that arise within them. The propositions follow particular themes, for example, in the case of religion, that natural events are under the control of unseen intentional agents (Barrett & Keil, 1996; Bering, 2011) to whom we may be accountable to in an afterlife (Solomon, Greenberg, & Pyszczynski, 2015) or, in the case of political ideologies, about the just ordering of economic relations and the extent to which the interests of kin should be prioritised over those of other groups (Haidt, 2013). Hence, the propositions within each network seem to orbit within the gravitational pull of more generalised dispositions towards the world that are rarely articulated and, therefore difficult to describe. Because these dispositions generate a repertoire of responses that can be called upon in almost any aspect of life, master interpretive systems are powerful organizational tools that can guide our actions in numerous situations and in the face of many different kinds of dilemmas, but at the cost of limiting human flexibility in exactly the way that Pavlov anticipated when describing the role of the second signalling system.

Religious belief systems, for example, provide models of the world and prescriptions for action (morality), coupled to a wide range of social practices which maintain these beliefs and which also have important social benefits (Geertz, 1966). The same is clearly true of political ideologies (Jost, Federico, & Napier, 2009); indeed, for much of human history, religious and political belief systems have been entwined to the point of being almost indistinguishable, only diverging in Europe following the French Revolution, a process which some social scientists think is now going into reverse (Micklethwait & Wooldridge, 2009). Conspiracy theories, which have often played a role in both religious and political discourse (Hofstadter, 1952), arguably also fall within this general class of master interpretive systems. Indeed, because individuals who believe in one conspiracy theory tend also to believe in others (even if they are contradictory; Wood, Douglas, & Sutton, 2012), psychological researchers have argued that conspiracist thinking cannot be to understood in terms of beliefs about specific conspiracies and should, instead, be considered a style of interpreting events in which nothing is assumed to be as it appears and world events are determined by secret, powerful institutions (Brotherton, 2015). The social element is perhaps less obvious than in the case of religious and political ideologies, although substantial social networks have arisen around some conspiracy theories (e.g. about the assassination of John F. Kennedy) and the recent proliferation of these beliefs via social media has created on-line echo chambers populated by networks of individuals who share similar convictions (Del Vicario et al., 2016).

Human beings typically define ourselves in terms of the groups to which we belong, a process known as social identification (Tajfel, 1979; Turner, Hogg, Oakes, Reicher, & Wetherell, 1987). People are capable of having multiple identities simultaneously; for example, I define myself as a father, a clinical psychologist, a university professor, British and also European. As a consequence of the human ability to assert ownership of beliefs, master interpretive systems are often co-opted for the purpose of identity-formation, so that we define ourselves as Marxists, Conservatives, Christians, Atheists and so on. Identifying with positively valued groups can enhance self-esteem and promote physical and mental health, an effect that is most evident when people identify with not one group but many (Haslam, Jetten, Postmes, & Haslam, 2009). However, identification can also lead to negative attitudes, sometimes extending to outright hostility directed towards competing out-groups, an effect that is most likely to occur if we embrace just one type of identity very strongly. This process appears to be one reason why religious and political fundamentalisms are sometimes associated with extreme violence (Herriot, 2007).

A curious feature of master interpretive systems, most clearly illustrated by political beliefs, is that the individual propositions that are their most visible manifestation may have little logical relation with each other. For example, the distinction between left and right ideologies (so described because, in the French National Assembly at the time of the Revolution, those who defended the Ancient Régime sat on the right whereas those who supported change sat on the left) seems to be universal (Jost et al., 2009) – conservatives on the right typically (although of course not always) endorse certain economic propositions (that the free market is the most just and effective way of organizing the economy) but also certain social values (support for the family, wariness or even hostility towards assigning equal rights for sexual minorities) and certain attitudes towards national defence (typically wanting high levels of funding for the armed forces). Leftists (again not invariably) support state interventions to redistribute wealth, equal rights for sexual minorities and advocate multilateral efforts to reduce the risk of military conflict. Bearing in mind my earlier point about the limitations of questionnaires, perhaps we could say that people on the right and the left tend to generate propositions reflecting these viewpoints but, of course, the precise nature of the propositions (the draft we take to be the 'true belief') will vary between individuals (conservatives may vary in their attitudes towards specific economic policies while agreeing about the broad benefits of a free market) and circumstances (someone on the left might advocate increased spending on the armed forces in support of peace enforcement missions).

Notice that there is no obvious reason why someone who advocates the free market should also be wary about gay rights or want to increase funding for the armed forces. What binds the relevant propositions must therefore be less visible, which is why we can be confident that master interpretive systems are organized around more generalised dispositions towards the world. Characterising these dispositions is, however, extremely difficult.

The Role of Implicit Processes in Master Interpretive Systems

Social psychologists, in particular, have made a number of attempts to classify the implicit processes underlying political and religious beliefs, for example arguing that they are related to a number of evolutionarily salient concerns such as the fear of death (Solomon et al., 2015), avoidance of uncertainty (Jost et al., 2009), or moral preferences relating to the care of others, fairness, loyalty, sanctity and the avoidance of contagion (Haidt, 2013). For each of these proposals, there is evidence that agreement with particular ideological and moral stances is associated with scores on relevant questionnaire measures (for example, that conservativism correlates with endorsement of statements about the importance of loyalty and indicative of extreme sensitivity to disgusting stimuli). In some cases, there is also evidence that 'priming' (prompting people to think about the relevant issues) produces shifts in the willingness to agree with particular viewpoints (for example, asking people to think about death tends make people endorse more extreme political views).

The problems with these accounts, it seems to me, is that they endeavour to capture within a verbal framework, processes that are largely non-verbal (indeed, this is precisely why they are said to be implicit). We therefore have a long way to go before we can characterise these processes accurately. At this stage of our understanding, it seems likely (as acknowledged by most existing accounts) that these processes have evolved to address fundamental biological and social needs common to at least all primate species, and that (as less often acknowledged) they are implemented by the associative system. To understand this idea, we can look briefly at the subtle role of disgust sensitivity in political beliefs.

Recall that one property of the associative system is that it allows organisms to assign positive or negative values to stimuli. It has long been known that mammalian species are evolutionarily prepared to learn disgust responses to noxious stimuli very quickly (a single pairing of a particular taste with a nausea-evoking stimulus can be sufficient to cause a life long aversion to whatever produced the taste; Garcia & Koelling, 1966). As already noted, numerous studies have shown that individuals who are more sensitive to disgust-related stimuli are more likely to be conservative and hostile to out-groups (Terrizzi, Shook, & McDaniel, 2013). One possible explanation for this association is that, in our evolutionary past, the disgust response has kept us apart from strangers who might be carriers of infection. Disgust also seems to be involved in concerns about 'purity' and the rejection of sexual minorities (whose preferences may be described as "filthy", "dirty" or, indeed, "disgusting") (Haidt, 2013). Indeed, when conservatives talk about their opposition to gay rights, a visceral disgust response is often all too obvious. Hence disgust sensitivity appears to be one factor that binds conservative attitudes together.

Speculating somewhat, I think it likely that specific implicit preferences, sustained by the associative system, play a role in all master interpretive systems. Indeed, as I will explain below, this is true not only of common master interpretive systems such as religious and political beliefs but also of delusional beliefs.

3.6 Resistance to Change

One of the most renown characteristics of delusions is their apparent resistance to change. As I noted earlier, this resistance may not be as remarkable as is often supposed (Brett-Jones et al., 1987; Colbert et al., 2010). Indeed, the cognitive behaviour therapy interventions that are now widely used to help patients with psychosis are specifically designed to reduce delusional conviction and are modestly effective in doing so (Turner, van der Gaag, Karyotaki, & Cuipers, 2014; Wykes, Steel, Everitt, & Tarrier, 2008). Hence, as I argued earlier, a mistaken impression of excessive delusional rigidity may have arisen as a consequence of comparing the beliefs of psychiatric patients with mundane beliefs; political and religious belief systems, which I have argued are a better comparison, are notoriously inflexible – it is rare that a political argument ends with one protagonist thumping their forehead and saying, "Doh! How could I have been so stupid?"

There are broadly two ways of explaining this kind of inflexibility, although they are not mutually exclusive. The first type of explanation appeals to the structure of master interpretive systems. As discussed earlier, their most important feature is that they do not consist of isolated propositions but, instead, should be thought of as groups of continually updated and interconnected propositions held together by the gravitational pull of implicit dispositions. Refuting any one proposition within a system of this kind will, in all likelihood, leave the remaining propositions untouched.

Even if this is not the case, it may be less cognitively effortful and more adaptive to shore up a propositional system with additional propositions if that system has served the individual well in the past. For this reason, true believers may decide that, "God moves in mysterious ways" or that the absence of evidence of a conspiracy is evidence of a conspiracy so profound that it leaves no evidence. (An interesting and historically significant real world example of the latter kind of reasoning occurred during the Reagan era, in 1976, when a CIA assessment of Russian nuclear capability concluded that they lacked an effective anti-ballistic missile system and, hence, that the Soviet government would not be able to survive a nuclear exchange. In response to the CIA's assessment, hawks within the Pentagon – who wished to justify increasing the US's nuclear arsenal – issued their own 'Team B' report, which concluded that the evidence presented by the CIA was so overwhelming and consistent that it could only be based on misinformation planted by Soviet agents (Rhodes, 2008)).

The second broad approach to explaining the rigidity of master interpretive systems appeals to emotional processes. As already noted, these systems are notorious for their ability to elicit strong emotional responses. Experimental studies confirm the everyday observation that, when people are presented with evidence that conflicts with their political convictions, they typically experience strong negative affect (Nisbett, Cooper, & Garrett, 2015), and expend considerable cognitive resources to finding reasons for rejecting or reinterpreting the evidence (Taber & Lodge, 2013; Westen, Blagov, Harenski, Hamann, & Kilts, 2006). The negative emotional consequences of encountering evidence that conflicts with pre-existing beliefs also helps to explain why, when seeking information about political issues (for example, when using online resources), people spend most of their time sampling information that is consistent with their beliefs while avoiding conflicting information (Knobloch-Westerwick & Meng, 2011).

The question of why evidence that is contrary to existing beliefs is experienced as emotionally toxic has not been sufficiently addressed by psychologists. However, it is probably a consequence of our tendency to claim ownership of our beliefs, and the investment we make in constructing them. Indeed, a recent experimental study found that establishing ownership of a theory in the most minimal way (by asking people to imagine that they had personally proposed it) was sufficient to increase confidence that the theory was correct (Gregg, Mahadevan, & Sedikides, 2017).

The more we claim ownership of a belief system, and the more we view our beliefs as badges of identity that bind us to others who share similar beliefs, the more likely it is that evidence contrary to our beliefs will be experienced as painful. When defending our beliefs, we are therefore, in some sense, defending ourselves.

3.7 Delusions as Master Interpretive Systems

Throughout this account I have pointed to various ways in which delusions resemble master interpretive systems. Like master interpretive systems, delusions generally follow particular themes which almost invariably reflect universal existential challenges (Musalek, Berner, & Katschnig, 1989) or concerns about the individual's position relative to others in the social world (Bentall, 1994), for example about the trustworthiness of others (paranoia), social status (grandiosity) or worthiness of the love (erotomania). By far the most common of these delusional systems is the paranoid system, in which the individual believes him or herself to be the victim of persecution by others (Bentall et al., 2001; Freeman, 2016). Of course, like other master interpretive systems, delusions are resistant (although not completely resistant) to counter-argument, and direct challenges to them often provoke strong negative affect.

Because paranoid delusions are so common, they have been subjected to more extensive research than any other types of delusional belief. Although there is insufficient space to review this research in detail here, a consistent finding in the literature is that these kinds of beliefs are associated with strong negative ideas about the self (Bentall et al., 2001; Freeman, 2016). However, by far the majority of studies of paranoia have focused on explicit cognitive processes such as self-esteem, and very little research has considered implicit processes. Here, I would like to suggest that, as seems to be the case for other master interpretive systems, implicit processes are also likely to be important. At this point it would be useful to consider some of my own most recent studies, which have examined the role of attachment processes in paranoia.

Since the work of John Bowlby (1969) it has been known that the intimate relationships that young children (and the infants of other mammalian species) form with their parents (or caregivers) provide a template for future adult relationships. Hence, depending on the quality of the relationships they experienced with caregivers during childhood, human adults have 'attachment styles' that may be secure (the assumption is that intimate relationships will be mutually supportive and beneficial) or, in various ways, insecure (the individual expects rejection or that other people will be untrustworthy). It is thought that specific attachment styles are associated with particular schemas or default beliefs about the self and others, so that secure attachment is associated with positive beliefs about the self and others and the insecure styles are associated with negative beliefs about the self, others, or both. Importantly, although developmental researchers have neglected the role of implicit, associative processes in attachment formation, they undoubtedly play a central role. In adults, attachments are often experienced as 'gut feelings'. Moreover, human infants form attachments very early – before they become fully verbal human beings – and non-verbal mammalian species are also capable of forming strong attachment relationships. Indeed, although dogs will never become jihadis, they form remarkably strong attachments to their human owners that mirror the attachments that human infants form towards their parents (Topál, Miklósi, Csányi, & Dóka, 1998). Hence, it is clear that language skills are not necessary in order for attachment relationships to be established.

For practical reasons, attachment styles are typically assessed in adult humans by means of questionnaires, and it is important to bear in mind the limitations of these kinds of measures discussed earlier earlier; in particular, although we may hope that these measures correlate with implicit processes they are not direct measures of those processes. These limitations notwithstanding, in my research I have found that insecure styles are strongly associated with paranoid beliefs in student samples (Pickering, Simpson, & Bentall, 2008), representative population samples (Sitko et al., 2014) and samples of psychiatric patients suffering from psychosis (Wickham, Sitko, & Bentall, 2015). Moreover, in epidemiological samples, attachment disrupting early life events, for example being neglected by parents or raised in a children's home, strongly predict the development of paranoid symptoms in later life (Bentall et al., 2012; Shevlin, McAnee, Bentall, & Murphy, 2015). Hence, there seems to be strong evidence that the disruption of attachment processes plays a causal role in paranoid delusions and, most likely, the relevant psychological mechanisms are at the implicit level.

Why Delusions Are Different: The Role of the Social[1]

Despite the important role of implicit dispositions in both widely held master interpretive systems and delusional beliefs, it is important to acknowledge that social factors are also important in shaping the precise

[1] I am grateful to Professor Tim Bayne for discussions that helped shape the ideas outlined in this section.

expression of these belief systems, particularly in the case of the former. For example, if we take the case of religious belief systems, it is obvious that children are not born Hindu, Christian, Muslim and so on. Developmental studies have shown that, although young children typically attribute intentionality to natural phenomena, they do not spontaneously assume the existence of a hidden creator (Banerjee & Bloom, 2013). Indeed, given the historical evidence that multiple deities preceded monotheistic systems in the evolution of religions (Wright, 2009), if children did spontaneously generate religious beliefs those beliefs would surely not be monotheistic.

Similarly, although studies of the developmental antecedents of ideology show that anxious children raised by authoritarian parents are especially likely to develop conservative attitudes in adulthood (Fraley, Griffin, Belsky, & Roisman, 2012), it is implausible that children are born with an innate wish to vote for a particular political party. The social environment, conversations with relatives and peers, and exposure to information in the media all play an important role. Our implicit dispositions constrain the kinds of interpretations of the world we find most congenial or, to repeat a metaphor I used earlier, act as a kind of centre of gravity around which beliefs plucked from a rich social market place of ideas can orbit and coalesce.

The recognition that the social world must be important in shaping master interpretive systems alerts us to a potentially important feature of delusional beliefs that is not obvious from the phenomenological data, and which is sometimes thought of as trivial. Delusions, in contrast to political and religious beliefs, are idiosyncratic. Indeed, some definitions of delusion, such as that in the earlier fourth edition of the American Psychiatric Association's diagnostic manual (APA, 1994), specifically exclude beliefs that "are ordinarily accepted by other members of the person's culture or subculture". Even when patients appear to have the same delusions (as in the famous case of the three patients who believed that they were Christ and who lived on the same ward at Ypsilati Hospital in the United States; Rokeach, 1964) the delusion is not really shared (each of the Ypsilati patients thought that the other two were deluded).

Usually, the idiosyncrasy of delusions is thought to be a consequence of their bizarreness – they seem so strange that no one but the deluded patient is convinced by them – but an intriguing possibility is that their asocial nature is both their defining feature and an important part of the causal pathway that leads to them. After all, in everyday life, we calibrate our beliefs according to the beliefs and reactions of those around us. As discussed earlier, what we believe to be factually the case is negotiated through interactions with other people, within discussions, and across multiple conversations conducted over extended periods of time (Edwards & Potter, 1992).

In the case of extreme political and religious beliefs – for example, Islamist extremism – this account is widely accepted, and lies behind attempts by intelligence services and governments to disrupt radical social networks, both in the actual and virtual worlds. Political radicalisation, just like religious radicalisation, is particularly likely to occur when the only social network that an individual encounters, and the only conversations that are heard, are all of a particular persuasion. Indeed, social psychological research confirms that people are more likely to develop extreme views when embedded in groups of like-minded people (Borum, 2011; Sunstein, 2009). The role of social identity in consolidating extremist beliefs, discussed earlier, adds to the danger that they will be translated into violent action (Herriot, 2007).

What I am suggesting here is that delusional beliefs may be different from radical beliefs, and perceived to be idiosyncratic by others, precisely because they are developed in isolation from any kind of conversation, or any kind of group to which the individual can refer to. In the absence of these kinds of conversations, there is no opportunity for consensus building or for beliefs to be challenged or modified by contrary views. Speculating further, it seems likely that this kind of isolation can occur for one or both of two separate reasons.

First, the person who develops beliefs that are later judged to be delusional may lack the cognitive and behavioural resources required to benefit from dialogue with other people. There are likely to be many psychological processes that contribute to the process of building a shared view of the world but one that is worth highlighting here is the capacity to understand the beliefs of other people, misleadingly described as having a 'theory of mind' after a celebrated article by Premack & Woodruff (1978). Numerous studies have reported impaired theory of mind skills in people with psychosis (Bora, Yucei, & Pantelis, 2009) with some evidence that this kind of impairment particularly contributes to paranoid delusions (Bentall et al., 2009).

Second, the individual may actually be isolated. There has been curiously little research into the quality and quantity of relationships experienced by people with psychosis, and that which has been carried out has often been conducted on the assumption that mental illness leads to social isolation. However, it is known that patients with positive symptoms of psychosis have impoverished social networks (Angell & Test, 2002) and that the same is true of people who are suffering the prodromal symptoms (sometimes called an at-risk-mental-state) that precede the onset of illness (Robustelli, Newberry, Whisman, & Mittal, 2017). Isolation also seems to be associated with psychotic symptoms in the general population (Butter, Murphy, Shevlin, & Houston, 2017) and, in a longitudinal study of Swedish army recruits, impoverished interpersonal relationships was found to predict future psychotic illness (Malmberg, Lewis, David, & Allebeck, 1998).

One important implication of these findings is that much more research needs to be conducted into the potential role of social isolation as a risk factor for psychosis and especially delusional beliefs.

3.8 Conclusion

In this chapter, I have attempted to create an account of what is involved when human beings have beliefs, and then explored the implications of this account for understanding delusions. It is worth restating that we have no warrant for assuming that the English language word 'belief' must pick out a specific type of psychological mechanism. Instead, I have tried to take what we know about human cognitive mechanisms to highlight those that provide the closest fit with our ordinary language use of the word 'belief'. This has led me to several conclusions.

First, there is no ultimate version or draft of what we believe that can be written down to make some kind of list. Instead, believing is something that we do online, in concert with other believers, a process that is constantly shaped by our interactions with others in our social world.

Second, the term belief should be restricted to propositions or verbal statements; although there is a lot that is belief-like going on in household pets, it would be wrong to say that animals believe.

Third, this claim notwithstanding, implicit or associative processes that we share with animals play an important role in constraining and shaping our beliefs. These implicit processes play a particularly important role in a class of belief phenomena that I have called master interpretive systems, which includes religious and political beliefs. These consist not of single propositions but of multiple propositions tied together by particular implicit dispositions that are related to fundamental human needs. I have suggested that the delusional beliefs of psychiatric patients are best compared to these master interpretive systems but differ from them in one important way: they occur in isolation and are not tested against the beliefs of other people.

Because delusions and master interpretive systems share many properties – particularly in respect to the underlying psychological processes and their resistance to change – it is reasonable to question the extent to which the two types of beliefs can be distinguished. Perhaps we should not be surprised by the troubles encountered when forensic practitioners attempt to make decisions about the culpability of apparently deluded offenders such as the Laffertys and Breivik. This is not to suggest that no differences can be discerned, of course, but that the distinction should not be thought of as binary.

More generally, I would like to suggest that psychopathologists might learn a lot by treating political and religious beliefs as analogues of the phenomena that they observe in the psychiatric clinic. It is striking that, to my knowledge, very little effort has been made by psychiatrists or clinical psychologists to consider the burgeoning literature in the psychology of religion or political psychology. It is even more remarkable that (despite the widespread use of the concept) there is no widely accepted psychological model of believing of the kind that I have tried to sketch out in this chapter.

References

Achen, C. H., & Bartels, L. M. (2016). *Democracy for realists: Why elections do not produce responsive government*. Princeton, NJ: Princeton University Press.

American Psychiatric Association. (1994). *Diagnostic and statistical manual for mental disorders* (4th ed.). Washington, DC: Author.

American Psychiatric Association. (2013). *Diagnostic and statistical manual for mental disorders* (5th ed.). Washington, DC: Author.

Angell, B., & Test, M. A. (2002). The relationship of clinical factors and environmental opportunities to social functioning in young adults with schizophrenia. *Schizophrenia Bulletin, 28*, 259–271.

Banerjee, K., & Bloom, P. (2013). Would Tarzan believe in god? Conditions for the emergence of religious belief. *Trends in Cognitive Science, 17*, 7–8.

Barrett, J. L., & Keil, F. C. (1996). Conceptualizing a nonnatural entity: Anthropomorphism in god concepts. *Cognitive Psychology, 31*, 219–247.

Bebbington, P., McBride, O., Steel, C., Kuipers, E., Radovanovič, M., Brugha, T., Jenkins, R., Meltzer, H.I. & Freeman, D. (2013). The structure of paranoia in the general population. *British Journal of Psychiatry, 202*, 419–427.

Beck, A. T. (1987). Cognitive models of depression. *Journal of Cognitive Psychotherapy: An International Quarterly, 1*, 5–37.

Bentall, R. P. (1994). Cognitive biases and abnormal beliefs: Towards a model of persecutory delusions. In A. S. David & J. Cutting (Eds.), *The neuropsychology of schizophrenia* (pp. 337–360). London: Lawrence Erlbaum.

Bentall, R. P., Corcoran, R., Howard, R., Blackwood, N., & Kinderman, P. (2001). Persecutory delusions: A review and theoretical integration. *Clinical Psychology Review, 21*, 1143–1192.

Bentall, R. P., Rowse, G., Shryane, N., Kinderman, P., Howard, R., Blackwood, N., Moore, R. & Corcoran, R. (2009). The cognitive and affective structure of paranoid delusions: A transdiagnostic investigation of patients with schizophrenia spectrum disorders and depression. *Archives of General Psychiatry, 66*, 236–247.

Bentall, R. P., Wickham, S., Shevlin, M., & Varese, F. (2012). Do specific early life adversities lead to specific symptoms of psychosis? A study from the 2007 The Adult Psychiatric Morbidity Survey. *Schizophrenia Bulletin, 38*, 734–740.

Bering, J. (2011). *The belief instinct*. New York: Norton.

Bora, E., Yucei, M., & Pantelis, C. (2009). Theory of mind impairment in schizophrenia: Meta-analysis. *Schizophrenia Research, 109*, 1–9.

Bortolotti, L. (2018). Delusion. In E. N. Zalta (Ed.), *The Stanford encyclopedia of philosophy*. Retrieved from https://plato.stanford.edu/archives/spr2018/entries/delusion/

Bortolotti, L., & Broome, M. (2012). Affective dimensions of the phenomenon of double bookkeeping delusions. *Emotion Review, 4*, 187–191.

Borum, R. (2011). Radicalization into violent extremism I: A review of social science theories. *Journal of Strategic Security, 4*, 7–36.

Bovet, P., & Parnas, J. (1993). Schizophrenic delusions: A phenomenological approach. *Schizophrenia Bulletin, 19*, 579–597.

Bowlby, J. (1969). *Attachment and loss: Vol 1 – Attachment*. London: Hogarth Press.

Brett-Jones, J., Garety, P., & Hemsley, D. (1987). Measuring delusional experiences: A method and its application. *British Journal of Clinical Psychology, 26*, 257–265.

Brewer, W. F. (1974). There is no convincing evidence for operant or classical conditioning in adult humans. In W. B. Weimer & D. S. Palermo (Eds.), *Cognition and symbolic processes* (pp. 1–42). Oxford, UK: Lawrence Erlbaum.

Brotherton, R. (2015). *Suspicious minds: Why we believe conspiracy theories*. London: Bloomsbury.

Butter, S., Murphy, J., Shevlin, M., & Houston, J. (2017). Social isolation and psychosis-like experiences: A UK general population analysis. *Psychosis, 9*, 291–300.

Churchland, P. S. (1986). *Neurophilosophy: Towards a unified science of the mind-brain*. Cambridge, MA: MIT Press.

Colbert, S. M., Peters, E. R., & Garety, P. A. (2010). Delusions and belief flexibility in psychosis. *Psychology and Psychotherapy: Theory, practice, research, 83*, 45–57.

Del Vicario, M., Bessi, A., Zollo, F., Petroni, F., Scala, A., Caldarelli, G., Stanley, H.E., & Quattrociocchi, W. (2016). The spreading of misinformation online. *Procedings of the National Academy of Science, 113*, 554–559.

Dennett, D. C. (1991). *Consciousness explained*. London: Allen Lane.

Edwards, D., & Potter, J. P. (1992). *Discursive psychology*. London: Sage.

Elahi, A., Parez-Algorta, G., Varese, F., McIntyre, J.C. & Bentall, R.P. (2017). Do paranoid delusions exist on a continuum with subclinical paranoia? A multi-method taxometric study. *Schizophrenia Research*. 190, 77–81.

Evans, J. S. B. T. (2008). Dual-process accounts of reasoning, judgment, and social cognition. *Annual Review of Psychology, 59*, 255–278.

Fernyhough, C. (2016). *The voices within*. London: Profile Books.

Fraley, R. C., Griffin, B. N., Belsky, J., & Roisman, G. I. (2012). Developmental antecedents of political ideology: A longitudinal investigation from birth to age 8 years. *Psychological Science, 23*, 1425–1431.

Freeman, D. (2016). Persecutory delusions: A cognitive perspective on understanding and treatment. *Lancet Psychiatry, 3*(7), 685–692.

Garcia, J., & Koelling, R. A. (1966). Relation of cue to consequence in avoidance learning. *Psychonomic Science, 4*, 123–124.

Gaston, S. (2018). *Citizen's voices: Insights from focus groups conducted in England for the project At Home in One's Past*. Retrieved from https://www.demos.co.uk/project/citizens-voices/

Gawronski, B., & Bodenhausen, G. V. (2006). Associative and propositional processes in evaluation: An integrative review of implicit and explicit attitude change. *Psychological Bulletin, 132*, 692–731.

Geertz, C. (1966). Religion as a cultural system. In M. Banton (Ed.), *Anthropological approaches to the study of religion* (pp. 1–46). London: Routledge.

Georgaca, E. (2000). Reality and discourse: A critical analysis of the category of 'delusions'. *British Journal of Medical Psychology, 73*, 227–242.

Gregg, A. P., Mahadevan, N., & Sedikides, C. (2017). The SPOT effect: People spontaneously prefer their own theories. *The Quarterly Journal of Experimental Psychology, 70*, 996–1010.

Haidt, J. (2013). *The righteous mind: Why good people are divided by politics and religion*. London: Allen Lane/The Penguin Press.

Hardy, A. (1979). *The spiritual nature of man: Study of contemporary religious experience*. Oxford, UK: Oxford University Press.

Haslam, S. A., Jetten, J., Postmes, T., & Haslam, C. (2009). Social identity, health and well-being: An emerging agenda for applied psychology. *Applied Psychology, 58*, 1–23.

Herriot, P. (2007). *Religious fundamentalism and social identity*. London: Routledge.
Hockett, C. F. (1959). Animal 'languages' and human language. *Human Biology, 31*, 32–39.
Hofstadter, R. (1952). *The paranoid style in American politics and other essays*. New York: Random House.
Janssen, I., Hanssen, M., Bak, M., Bijl, R. V., De Graaf, R., Vollenberg, W., McKenzie, K., & van Os, J. (2003). Discrimination and delusional ideation. *British Journal of Psychiatry, 182*, 71–76.
Jaspers, K. (1913/1963). *General psychopathology* (J. Hoenig & M. W. Hamilton, Trans.). Manchester, UK: Manchester University Press.
Jost, J. T., Federico, C. M., & Napier, J. L. (2009). Political ideology: Its structure, functions, and elective affinities. *Annual Review of Psychology, 60*, 307–337.
Kahneman. (2012). *Thinking, fast and slow*. London: Penguin.
Knobloch-Westerwick, S., & Meng, J. (2011). Reinforcement of the political self through selective exposure to political messages. *Journal of Communication, 61*, 349–368.
Krakauer, J. (2003). *Under the banner of heaven: A story of violent faith*. New York: Doubleday.
Luhrmann, T. (2012). *When God talks back: Understanding the American evangelical relationship with God*. New York: Random House.
Lyn, H. (2012). Apes and the evolution of language: Taking stock of 40 years of research. In J. Vonk & T. K. Shackelford (Eds.), *The Oxford handbook of comparative evolutionary psychology* (pp. 356–377). Oxford, UK: Oxford University Press.
MacCulloch, D. (2009). *A history of Christianity: The first three thousand years*. London: Penguin.
Malmberg, A., Lewis, G., David, A., & Allebeck, P. (1998). Premorbid adjustment and personality in people with schizophrenia. *British Journal of Psychiatry, 172*, 308–313.
Martin, A. (2009). Semantic memory. In L. R. Squire (Ed.), *Encyclopedia of neuroscience* (pp. 561–566). Amsterdam: Elsevier.
McPhail, E. M. (1982). *Brain and intelligence in vertebrates*. Oxford, UK: Clarendon Press.
Melle, I. (2013). The Breivik case and what psychiatrists can learn from it. *World Psychiatry, 12*, 16–21.
Micklethwait, J., & Wooldridge, A. (2009). *God is back: How the global rise in faith is changing the world*. London: Penguin.
Mitchell, C. J., de Houwer, J., & Lovibond, P. (2009). The propositional nature of human learning. *Behavioral and Brain Sciences, 32*, 183–246.
Musalek, M., Berner, P., & Katschnig, H. (1989). Delusional theme, sex and age. *Psychopathology, 22*, 260–267.

Nisbett, E. C., Cooper, K. E., & Garrett, R. K. (2015). The partisan brain: How dissonant science messages lead conservatives and liberals to (dis)trust science. *Annals of the American Academy of Political and Social Science, 658*, 36–66.

Parnas, J. (2013). The Breivik case and "conditio psychiatrica". *World Psychiatry, 12*, 22–23.

Parnas, J., Handest, P., Jansson, L., & Sæbye, D. (2005). Anomalous subjective experience among first-admitted schizophrenia spectrum patients: Empirical investigation. *Psychopathology, 38*, 259–267.

Pavlov, I. P. (1941). *Conditioned reflexes and psychiatry* (W. H. Gantt, Trans.). New York: International Publishers.

Pearce, J. M. (2008). *Animal learning and cognition: An introduction*. Hove, UK: Psychology Press.

Pepperberg, I. M. (2017). Animal language studies: What happened? *Psychonomic Bulletin and Review, 24*, 181–185.

Piaget, J. (1926). *The language and thought of the child*. London: Routledge and Kegan Paul.

Pickering, L., Simpson, J., & Bentall, R. P. (2008). Insecure attachment predicts proneness to paranoia but not hallucinations. *Personality and Individual Differences, 44*, 1212–1224.

Premack, D., & Woodruff, G. (1978). Does the chimpanzee have a theory of mind? *Behavioural and Brain Sciences, 4*, 515–526.

Reber, A. S. (1989). Implicit learning and tacit knowledge. *Journal of Experimental Psychology: General, 118*, 219–235.

Rhodes, R. (2008). *Arsenals of folly: The making of the nuclear arms race*. London: Simon and Schuster.

Robustelli, B. L., Newberry, R. E., Whisman, M. A., & Mittal, V. A. (2017). Social relationships in young adults at ultra high risk for psychosis. *Psychiatry Research, 247*, 345–351.

Rokeach, M. (1964). *The three Christs of Ypsilanti: A psychological study*. London: Arthur Baker.

Sass, L. A. (1994). *The paradoxes of delusion: Wittgenstein, Schreber and the schizophrenic mind*. Ithaca, NY: Cornell University Press.

Sass, L. A. (2014). Delusions and double book-keeping. In T. Fuchs, T. Breyer, & C. Mundt (Eds.), *Karl Jaspers' philosophy and psychopathology* (pp. 125–148). New York: Springer.

Schreber, D. (1903/1955). *Memoirs of my nervous illness* (I. Macalpine & R. A. Hunter, Trans.). London: Dawsons.

Schwitzgebel, E. (2015). Belief. *Stanford encyclopedia of philosophy*. Retrieved from https://plato.stanford.edu/archives/sum2015/entries/belief/

Shevlin, M., McAnee, G., Bentall, R. P., & Murphy, K. (2015). Specificity of association between adversities and the occurrence and co-occurrence paranoia and hallucinations: Evaluating the stability of risk in an adverse adult environment. *Psychosis, 7*, 206–216.

Sitko, K., Bentall, R. P., Shevlin, M., O'Sullivan, N., & Sellwood, W. (2014). Associations between specific psychotic symptoms and specific childhood adversities are mediated by attachment styles: An analysis of the National Comorbidity Survey. *Psychiatry Research, 217*, 202–209.

Skinner, B. F. (1945). The operational analysis of psychological terms. *Psychological Review, 52*, 270–277.

Solomon, S., Greenberg, J., & Pyszczynski, T. (2015). *The worm at the core: The role of death in life*. London: Penguin.

Sperber, D. (2000). Metarepresentations in an evolutionary peespective. In D. Sperber (Ed.), *Metarepresentations: A multidisciplinary perspective* (pp. 117–138). Oxford, UK: Oxford University Press.

Stich, S. (1996). *Deconstructing the mind*. Oxford, UK: Oxford University Press.

Sunstein, C. R. (2009). *Going to extremes: How like minds unite and divide*. Oxford, UK: Oxford University Press.

Taber, C. S., & Lodge, M. (2013). *The rationalizing voter*. Cambridge, MA: Cambridge University Press.

Tajfel, H. (1979). Indivuduals and groups in social psychology. *British Journal of Social and Clinical Psychology, 18*, 183–190.

Terrace, H. S., Petitto, L. A., Sanders, R. J., & Bever, T. G. (1979). Can an ape create a sentence? *Science, 206*, 891–902.

Terrizzi, J. A., Shook, N. J., & McDaniel, M. A. (2013). The behavioral immune system and social conservatism: A meta-analysis. *Evolution and Human Behavior, 34*, 99–108.

Topál, J., Miklósi, Á., Csányi, V., & Dóka, A. (1998). Attachment behavior in dogs (Canis familiaris): A new application of Ainsworth's (1969) Strange Situation Test. *Journal of Comparative Psychology, 112*, 219–229.

Turner, D. T., van der Gaag, M., Karyotaki, E., & Cuipers, P. (2014). Psychological interventions for psychosis: A meta-analysis of comparative outcome studies. *American Journal of Psychiatry*. https://doi.org/10.1176/appi.ajp.2013.13081159

Turner, J. C., Hogg, M. A., Oakes, P. J., Reicher, S. D., & Wetherell, M. S. (1987). *Rediscovering the social group: A self-categorization theory*. Oxford, UK: Blackwell.

Vygotsky, L. S. V. (1962). *Thought and language*. Cambidge, MA: MIT Press.

Wagner, A. R., & Rescorla, R. (1972). Inhibition in Pavlovian conditioning: Applications of a theory. In R. A. Boakes & M. S. Halliday (Eds.), *Inhibition and learning* (pp. 301–336). New York: Academic.

Watson, J. B. (1924). *Behaviorism*. New York: Norton.

Weiner, B. (2008). Reflections on the history of attribution theory and research: People, personalities, publications, problems. *Social Psychology, 39*, 151–156.

Westen, D., Blagov, P. S., Harenski, K., Hamann, S., & Kilts, C. (2006). Neural bases of motivated reasoning: An fMRI study of emotional contraints on partisan political judgment in the 2004 US Presidential Election. *Journal of Cognitive Neuroscience, 18*, 1947–1958.
Wickham, S., Sitko, K., & Bentall, R. P. (2015). Insecure attachment is associated with paranoia but not hallucinations in psychotic patients: The mediating role of negative self esteem. *Psychological Medicine, 45*, 1495–1507.
Winch, P. (1958). *The idea of a social science in relation to philosophy*. London: Routledge.
Wittgenstein, L. (1953). *Philosophical investigations*. London: Blackwell.
Wolfe, T. (2016). *The kingdom of speech*. London: Jonathan Cape.
Wood, M. J., Douglas, K. M., & Sutton, R. M. (2012). Dead and alive: Beliefs in contradictory conspiracy theories. *Social Psychological and Personality Science, 3*, 767–773.
Wright, R. (2009). *The evolution of God*. London: Little Brown.
Wykes, T., Steel, C., Everitt, B. S., & Tarrier, N. (2008). Cognitive behavior therapy for schizophrenia: Effect sizes, clinical models, and methodological rigor. *Schizophrenia Bulletin, 34*, 523–527.
Yang, C. (2013). The ontogeny and phylogeny of language. *Procedings of the National Academy of Science, 110*, 6324–6327.

CHAPTER 4

Delusions and Three Myths of Irrational Belief

Lisa Bortolotti

Abstract This chapter addresses the contribution that the delusion literature has made to the philosophy of belief. Three conclusions will be drawn: (1) a belief does not need to be epistemically rational to be used in the interpretation of behaviour; (2) a belief does not need to be epistemically rational to have significant psychological or epistemic benefits; (3) beliefs exhibiting the features of epistemic irrationality exemplified by delusions are not infrequent, and they are not an exception in a largely rational belief system. What we learn from the delusion literature is that there are complex relationships between rationality and interpretation, rationality and success, and rationality and knowledge.

In the preparation of this chapter, Lisa Bortolotti acknowledges the support of project PERFECT, funded by a European Research Council Consolidator Award (grant agreement 616358). She is also grateful to Martin Davies and Matthew Broome for teaching her about delusions.

L. Bortolotti (✉)
Philosophy Department and Institute for Mental Health, University of Birmingham, Birmingham, UK
e-mail: L.Bortolotti@bham.ac.uk

L. Bortolotti (ed.), *Delusions in Context*,
https://doi.org/10.1007/978-3-319-97202-2_4

Keywords Delusion • Belief • Rationality • Epistemic functionality • Psychological wellbeing • Mental health • Success • Sense of agency

4.1 Lessons from Delusions

In recent years, the focus on delusions in the philosophical literature has contributed to dispel some myths about belief, making room for a more psychologically realistic picture of the mind. What do we know about delusions that can inform our understanding of how beliefs are adopted and maintained, and how they influence behaviour? What have philosophers learnt from delusions? An entire volume could be dedicated to this issue alone, but in this chapter I will focus on three core philosophical claims about epistemically irrational beliefs that our knowledge of delusions have successfully challenged.

First, our beliefs do not need to be epistemically rational to be used in the attempt to interpret our behaviour. The ascription of an epistemically irrational belief to us often contributes to the process of explaining and predicting what we do. Second, our beliefs do not need to be epistemically rational to have a positive impact on our psychological wellbeing or understanding. Sometimes, an epistemically irrational belief has some long- or short-term epistemic benefit because it shields us from anxiety or supports our sense of agency. Third, beliefs exhibiting the features of epistemic irrationality exemplified by delusions are not infrequent, and they are not an exception. Optimistically biased beliefs about ourselves, for instance, may also be poorly supported by the evidence available to us, and resistant to the evidence that becomes available to us at a later stage. Yet, they are very common and widely regarded as adaptive. This suggests that epistemic irrationality cannot account for the pathological nature of delusions.

In discussions about interdisciplinary projects involving philosophers, it is not uncommon to identify the role of the philosopher with the conceptual tidying up and clarifying that are often deemed to be necessary in complex empirical investigations, or with the capacity to place a timely investigation within a wider historical context. By all means, such roles are important and philosophers are well placed to assist. However, as others have observed (e.g., Fulford, Stanghellini, & Broome, 2004), the role of the philosopher does not need to be so narrowly confined. Philosophers can also help develop a field in a certain direction, offering hypotheses to test and examining the wider implications of existing empirical results.

In this chapter, I want to focus not on what philosophy can do for psychology and psychiatry, but on what psychology and psychiatry have done for philosophy. As I hope to show, there are opportunities for philosophers who engage in interdisciplinary projects to learn something from the empirical and clinical sciences about the nature of those phenomena that have traditionally been at the centre of philosophical investigation. A careful analysis of the results of focused empirical work on the relevant phenomena, and attention to detail in the relevant case studies can reveal the inadequacy of established philosophical theories and suggest new ways of looking at things.

Here I provide an example of this. I argue that the study of delusions has contributed to challenging some widely accepted assumptions in the philosophy of mind concerning the relationship between epistemic rationality and belief.

Although definitions of delusions vary to some extent, most definitions are based on the surface features of the delusions, and identify delusions as *epistemically irrational beliefs*. Let's see what it means for a delusion to be a belief that is epistemically irrational. First, what is a *belief*? Whereas our desire tells us how we would like things to be, our belief tells us how we take things to be. Thus, a belief is a mental state that purports to represent reality. If I believe that it rarely snows in London, I am committed to the truth of the claim that it rarely snows in London. Typically, our beliefs manifest in our verbal and non-verbal behaviour. For instance, I may decide that it is not a good idea to buy snow boots if I am going to spend most of the winter in London.

There are several distinct accounts of epistemic irrationality in the philosophical literature, but the central idea is that epistemic irrationality concerns the relationship between a belief and the evidence for it.[1] The notion of epistemic irrationality I am going to work with for the purposes of this chapter is as follows: we are epistemically irrational when (1) we do not have evidence supporting our beliefs prior to adopting them; or (2) we are not responsive to evidence against our beliefs that becomes available to us after their adoption.

[1] See for instance: "By *epistemic* rationality, I mean, roughly, the kind of rationality which one displays when one believes propositions that are strongly supported by one's evidence and refrains from believing propositions that are improbable given one's evidence" (Kelly, 2003, p. 612).

According to some of the most influential definitions in the clinical and empirical literature, delusions are epistemically irrational beliefs.[2] One good example of this general trend is the definition we find in the *Diagnostic and Statistical Manual of Mental Disorders* (DSM). The DSM-V says that delusions are "based on incorrect inference about external reality that are firmly sustained despite what almost everyone else believes and despite what constitutes incontrovertible and obvious proof or evidence to the contrary" (APA, 2013). The definition has been rightly criticised for the terminology it uses (Are all delusions *based on inference*? Can beliefs be *proven* to be false?) and for other good reasons (e.g., Coltheart, 2007, p. 1043), but it captures some aspects of the nature of delusions. In particular, both features of epistemic irrationality are present in the definition: delusions are ill-grounded and are not abandoned in the face of obvious proof or evidence against them.

If delusions are epistemically irrational beliefs, then they will share the characteristics typically attributed to epistemically irrational beliefs. But do they?

I will focus on three claims that are often regarded as safe assumptions about epistemically irrational beliefs in the philosophy of mind, and ask to what extent they are true of delusions. The first claim is that, due to our epistemically irrational beliefs, our behaviour is either impossible or difficult to understand, and other people's attempts to interpret or predict our actions on the basis of our beliefs are destined to fail. The second claim is that our epistemically irrational beliefs have negative consequences for our psychological and epistemic status, by compromising both our wellbeing and our access to the truth, and thus they should be challenged by default. The third claim is that epistemically irrational beliefs are an anomaly to be explained away, an exception in our largely rational belief system. Indeed, it is only because epistemic irrationality is not widespread that we can have intentional agency at all.

I will argue in this chapter that the three claims about epistemically irrational beliefs are not compatible with what we know about delusions. Moreover, they are inaccurate and misleading when applied to a number

[2] See for instance: "A person is deluded when they have come to hold a particular belief with a degree of firmness that is both utterly unwarranted by the evidence at hand, and that jeopardises their day-to-day functioning" (McKay et al., 2005, p. 315) and: "Delusions are generally accepted to be beliefs which (a) are held with great conviction; (b) defy rational counter-argument; and (c) would be dismissed as false or bizarre by members of the same socio-cultural group" (Gilleen & David, 2005, pp. 5–6).

of beliefs that are commonly regarded as epistemically irrational but are not delusional. In other words, they are either claims that must be qualified, or myths that must be left behind.

In Sects. 4.2 and 4.3, I explain how the study of delusions shows not only that epistemically irrational beliefs can be understood, but that it is often via the attribution of those beliefs to us that our behaviour can be explained and predicted. Even so-called 'bizarre delusions' can be understood in context and appealed to, both in the explanation of past behaviour and in the prediction of future behaviour. Thus, it is implausible to hold that epistemically irrational beliefs always or by necessity compromise interpretation.

In Sects. 4.4, 4.5 and 4.6, I offer some reasons to qualify the claim that irrational beliefs have negative consequences from a psychological and epistemic point of view. In some cases, irrational beliefs can have significant psychological and even epistemic benefits. In particular, delusional beliefs have some (obvious, long-term) costs and some (less obvious, shorter-term) benefits. Delusions appear not to be well-supported by evidence, are resistant to counterevidence and counterargument, and can seriously disrupt functioning. Depending on their content, they can be a source of anxiety and distress. But they can also make a contribution to our sense of competence and coherence, and, in the critical situation in which they often emerge, they can even support our engagement with the surrounding physical and social environment after uncertainty, trauma, or abuse. Thus, as counter-intuitive as it may sound, in those circumstances it may be unwise to challenge delusions.

Although philosophers accept that some false and irrational beliefs can be useful in some contexts, they are very resistant to the idea that false and irrational beliefs might have some positive role to play from an epistemic point of view. Surely, false and irrational beliefs take us further from the truth. How can they contribute to the achievement of epistemic goals, such as the acquisition, retention, and use of relevant information? I will show that some false and irrational beliefs can play a positive epistemic function. In particular, some delusions serve as an emergency response to a break-down of epistemic functionality.

In Sect. 4.7, I challenge the claim that irrational beliefs are the exception to the rule, a relatively rare occurrence in our largely rational belief systems. Although clinically significant delusions are not widespread, beliefs sharing the same epistemic features as delusions, and thus falling short of standards of epistemic rationality, are common. Here I will refer to positive illusions (Taylor, 1989) generating overly optimistic beliefs about ourselves that are not well-supported by evidence, are resistant to counterevidence, and often misrepresent reality. What distinguishes delusions from optimistically biased beliefs and other epistemically irrational beliefs is an interesting question that has not been satisfactorily answered yet. But the discussion in this chapter will give us reason to believe that the source of the alleged pathological nature of delusions cannot be their epistemic irrationality.

In Sect. 4.8, I will examine the implications of dispelling the three myths of epistemically irrational belief discussed in the previous sections. How does the rejection of the assumptions surrounding epistemically irrational beliefs affect what we know about the mind and how we view mental health?

4.2 "Irrational Beliefs Make Interpretation Impossible"

If a man says that there is a full-scale nuclear reactor inside himself, or if a woman says that she is always pregnant and giving birth to a series of Messiahs, you may wonder whether they really mean what they say.[3] That is because what these people say sounds not just implausible, but *impossible*.

On an influential view in philosophy of mind, rationality and understanding go hand in hand. More precisely, our behaviour can be interpreted, explained, and predicted *in intentional terms*, that is, by reference to our beliefs, desires, intentions, and so on, only if it meets some basic standards of rationality. The view is reflected in two influential approaches to interpretation, the so-called *principle of charity* (Davidson, 1980) and the *intentional stance* (Dennett, 1987).

> If we are intelligibly to attribute attitudes and beliefs, or usefully to describe motions as behavior, then we are committed to finding, in the pattern of behavior, belief, and desire, a large degree of rationality and consistency. (Davidson, 1980, p. 237)

> When we are not [rational], the cases defy description in ordinary terms of belief and desire. (Dennett, 1987, p. 87)

[3] These examples are discussed in Bortolotti and Broome (2012).

Although for Davidson and Dennett the demands of epistemic rationality do not exhaust the rationality constraints on belief attribution, epistemic rationality plays a central role in the development of their views on belief and intentionality.

There are several versions of the idea that rationality and interpretation go together, some stronger (according to which *it is impossible* to interpret irrational behaviour) and other weaker (according to which *it is especially difficult* to interpret irrational behaviour). Here is one version of the idea that there is a rationality constraint on the ascription of beliefs:

> Propositional attitudes have their proper home in explanations of a special sort: explanations in which things are made intelligible by being revealed to be, or to approximate to being, as they rationally ought to be. (McDowell, 1985, p. 389)

4.3 Bizarre Delusions

So-called *bizarre* delusions seem to be the perfect illustration of the claim that irrationality compromises interpretation and understanding. In the DSM-V, delusions are described as bizarre "if they are clearly implausible and not understandable to same-culture peers and do not derive from ordinary life experiences" (APA, 2013). 'Bizarre' delusions are epistemically irrational in that they are neither well-supported by the existing evidence, nor responsive to new evidence; moreover, they are *implausible*, typically conflicting with other things we are committed to.[4]

Karl Jaspers (1963) describes some delusions (those delusions that involve a radical transformation of both experience and meaning) as *ununderstandable*. The definition of delusions in the DSM-V (APA, 2013, p. 87) reflects this approach: bizarre delusions are an instance of irrational behaviour ("fixed beliefs that are not amenable to change in light of conflicting evidence") that cannot be interpreted ("clearly implausible and not understandable to same-culture peers").

But the view that our behaviour cannot be interpreted in intentional terms unless the belief we seem to express is rational has unattractive

[4] See for instance: "Rationality is a normative constraint of consistency and coherence on the formation of a set of beliefs and thus is prima facie violated in two ways by the delusional subject. First she accepts a belief that is incoherent with the rest of her beliefs, and secondly she refuses to modify that belief in the face of fairly conclusive counterevidence and a set of background beliefs that contradict the delusional belief" (Gerrans, 2000, p. 114).

consequences. If we cannot be interpreted as believing what we say, and our behaviour cannot be explained or predicted on the basis of our reports, when they are taken literally, then what should our interpreters do?

They could attempt to *rationalise* what we say, that is, assume that we do not mean what we literally say. As a result, they could make an alternative attribution to us that no longer violates rationality constraints. They could make sense of the man reporting that he has a nuclear reactor inside himself by 'correcting' his report: "Maybe, what he means is that *he feels like* he has a reactor inside himself because he feels that there is something wrong with him." The same strategy of rationalisation could be adopted in the case of the woman reporting that she has given birth to an endless series of Messiahs. "Maybe, what she means is that *she is willing to* give birth to an endless series of Messiahs if God asks her to, because she want to do God's will."

In cases of apparent irrationality, philosophers committed to there being a rationality constraint on belief ascription suggest that interpreters need to find a way to rationalise the report, to 'correct the mistake'.[5] The problem is that the rest of the behaviour of people with 'bizarre' delusions often makes sense only if their reports are taken at face value, literally, and not as metaphorical expressions of discomfort or desire. It is because the content of the delusion is believed, often with conviction, that it has such a significant, and often disruptive, impact on their lives.

The man who reported that he had a nuclear reactor inside himself *was concerned* about the presence of the nuclear reactor, and *experienced frustration* when others did not believe him. The man would not have been as concerned if the presence of a reactor inside himself had just been a metaphor, and he would not have felt frustration at other people's disbelief. The woman who reported that she had given birth to an endless series of Messiahs *felt privileged* about her condition (Bortolotti & Broome, 2012, p. 190). The woman would not have felt this way if she had just desired to give birth to Messiahs. It is because she believed that she had given birth to them that she felt privileged.

The strong feelings and persistent thoughts related to our 'bizarre' delusions are easier to understand in the context of our *believing* (as opposed

[5] See for instance: "[…] when a mistake is agreed to have been made we will often look for, and find, a reason why it was made, not just in the sense of cause or regularity in its making but in the sense of some excuse which reconciles the mistake with the idea that, even in making it, the perpetrator was exercising his or her rationality" (Heal, 1998, p. 99).

to *imagining* or *desiring*) that we are in a very peculiar situation. And the content of the delusional beliefs may not appear as *bizarre* in the context of our experiences prior to the adoption of the delusional beliefs. In many circumstances delusions make sense. For instance, those who develop delusions of persecution often have been abused or mistreated in their past and so their tendency to see other people as hostile can be easily explained in context (see Gunn & Bortolotti, 2018).

Some background knowledge about our significant life events combined with attention to how we talk about our experiences can help the interpreter make sense of 'bizarre' delusions. This idea can be extended to a wider range of unusual beliefs. For instance, it is easier to understand why we claim to have been abducted by aliens if interpreters take into account our experiences and cultural background (see Bortolotti, Gunn, & Sullivan-Bissett, 2016). Experiences of 'abduction' can be caused by a phenomenon called 'awareness during sleep paralysis' (ASP) and by hypnopompic hallucinations. During Rapid Eye Movement (REM) sleep, we are immobilized and can wake up before the paralysis has disappeared, realising that we are unable to move. Sleep paralysis can be accompanied by hypnopompic hallucinations, which means that we are also hallucinating sights and sounds. Faced with these experiences, we search for an explanation, and we may be inclined to believe that we have been abducted by aliens if we belong to a sub-culture where the idea of intelligent aliens coming in contact with humans is not ruled out.

4.4 "Irrational Beliefs Are Always Bad for Us"

Delusional beliefs are a common example of irrationality but are also a perfect illustration of beliefs that can be *harmful*, generating distress, and severely disrupting our lives. Many of the people who come to the attention of healthcare professionals and are diagnosed with delusions do not sleep properly, experience social withdrawal, cannot keep their jobs or continue their studies, and cause concern to their families, employers, neighbours, sometimes even the police.

Although there are cases where some people feel at least temporarily empowered by or privileged about the content of their delusions (as the woman who thought she had given birth to an endless series of Messiahs), for the great majority of people delusions are a source of unhappiness. Thus, it is natural to link the epistemic irrationality of the delusions to their harmfulness. Isn't it because they are so divorced from reality that delusions end up affecting our lives so negatively? I hope to show here that the link between harmfulness and epistemic irrationality is tempting, but is ultimately an oversimplification.

I am going to offer some examples of delusions that are harmful, in that they generate clashes with reality that are a source of anxiety and distress, but also play a protective or defensive role, temporarily ameliorating a critical situation. Let's start with the most obvious example, so-called *motivated* delusions (Bortolotti, 2015). How the delusions are described gives it away: these are beliefs that we may be motivated to hold on to, because they represent not the reality we find ourselves in, but a reality we would prefer to be in.

4.5 Motivated Delusions

An example of a delusion with a defensive function is the case of Reverse Othello syndrome detailed in P.V. Butler and further discussed by Ryan McKay, Robyn Langdon, and Max Coltheart. BX was a talented musician who became quadriplegic after a tragic accident. He believed that he was still in a satisfying relationship, when in fact the woman who had been his partner had left him and started a relationship with someone else (McKay, Langdon, & Coltheart, 2005). BX's belief in the fidelity of his former partner and the continued success of his relationship was very resistant to counterevidence. BX believed that his relationship was going well, even though his former partner refused to communicate with him (Butler, 2000, p. 86).

The Reverse Othello syndrome can be seen as a special case of erotomania. In erotomania, we come to believe that another person, often of a perceived higher status, is in love with us when there is no clear evidence in support of that belief. Here is a more typical case of erotomania. LT was a young woman who became obsessed with the idea that a fellow student was in love with her although the two had never spoken to each other. She explained that the student would send her love messages and marriage proposals via the TV, the colours of dresses, and car licence plates (Jordan & Howe, 1980). Although the young man was asked to talk to LT on the phone, clarifying that he had no intention to marry her, LT remained convinced that he loved her, and came to believe that the man on the phone was another person.

In the cases of BX and LT, what are their delusions protecting them from? It is not easy to say, but one can speculate from the further details provided in the case studies. Butler argues that for BX the appearance of the delusion "may mark an adaptive attempt to regain intrapsychic coherence and to confer meaning on otherwise catastrophic loss or emptiness" (Butler, 2000, p. 90). BX did feel a sense of loss after the accident because he acquired a severe disability compromising his future aspirations. The belief that his relationship had not ended was both false and resistant to counterevidence, but gave him hope and strength at a critical time.

LT's mother described her as quiet and lonely, and explained that one of her brief relationships had ended just before she started believing that her fellow student was in love with her. The break up had caused her significant distress (Jordan & Howe, 1980, pp. 982–3). The belief that she was loved and desired might have protected LT from low mood, following a long history of low self-esteem and a recent, painful rejection.

The lesson from motivated delusions is that an epistemically irrational belief can prevent people who have experienced traumatic or emotionally distressing events from becoming depressed. As the belief enhances reality, in the short run it may be a psychologically adaptive response. By enabling us to continue to interact with the surrounding environment (albeit imperfectly), motivated delusions can also support our epistemic functionality, that is, our capacity to acquire, retain, and use relevant information. Along these lines, Butler and his team speculated that BX's Reverse Othello syndrome supported his motivation to engage in rehabilitation, and noted that the delusion faded away soon after the rehabilitation programme had ended.

The adoption of motivated delusions seems to provide some temporary relief from low mood and anxiety and thus protecting from lack of concentration, irritability, social isolation, and emotional disturbances. One might think that the case of motivated delusions is especially well suited to the purpose of showing that some epistemically irrational beliefs can be good for us. But it has been suggested that other types of delusions can also play an adaptive role, at least in the short term.

4.6 Delusions in Schizophrenia

Consider the following example, adapted from the one originally presented by Schneider in *Clinical Psychopathology* (1959). You are taking a walk in your hometown when you notice a dog on the steps of a Catholic church. While you pass the front of the church, the dog gets up on his hind legs. Then he moves his front paw forward. What do you make of this? Probably nothing. But what if you felt that the dog's action was meant for you? Maybe you would start thinking about other events involving churches that you witnessed recently. Maybe the previous encounters were also meant for you and led up to today's event. Maybe the dog was trying to communicate something. Maybe he was delivering a message from God, revealing that you were chosen to carry out an important mission.

The hypothesis that the dog is a messenger from God is far-fetched, you can grant that. If one of your friends had come up with such a story you would not believe her, and so it is not a surprise for you if your friends do not believe you when you tell them. But you just *know* it is true. It explains everything. Knowing why the dog behaved as he did dissolves at last the anxiety and uncertainty that had become a constant feature of your everyday experiences: feeling that something important was about to happen, and the dread of not knowing what it was. When you realize that the dog is delivering a message from God, you feel relieved and empowered. God has found a secret and effective way to communicate with you.

Classical authors such as Karl Jaspers (Jaspers, 1963) and Klaus Conrad (Mishara, 2010), and contemporary authors such as Glen Roberts (Roberts, 1991, 2006), and Aaron Mishara and Phil Corlett (Mishara & Corlett, 2009), have argued that elaborated delusions in schizophrenia can be seen as either an emergency response or a revelation, putting an end to a situation of great uncertainty and anxiety. To start with, the adoption of a delusional hypothesis may support epistemic functionality by fostering a new attitude towards experience. We feel that it is in our power to understand what is going on in our lives. An interesting study (Bergstein, Weizman, & Solomon, 2008) has shown that people with elaborated delusions in the acute stage of psychosis have a strong *sense of coherence*, a psychological construct encompassing intellectual curiosity and a sense of self-efficacy and purpose.[6] Arguably, such an attitude towards experience is more conducive to the acquisition and exchange of information than the state of passive, anxious uncertainty that characterizes the prodromal phase of psychosis.

[6] The sense of coherence is defined as "a global orientation that expresses the extent to which one has a pervasive, enduring though dynamic, feeling of confidence that (1) the stimuli deriving from one's internal and external environments are structured, predictable, and explicable; (2) the resources are available to one to meet the demands posed by these stimuli; and (3) these demands are challenges, worthy of investment and engagement" (Antonovsky, 1987, p. 91).

Then, the adoption of the delusion may have positive effects on the habitual and automated processes that are conducive to learning. One common view about the adoption of delusional beliefs is that, in the prodromal stage of psychosis, we experience random events as especially important to us and cannot understand why.[7] Such experiences can become distressing and demand an explanation (such as, "God is using the dog to send me a message"). The delusion can be that explanation, enabling us to overcome uncertainty and making sense of what goes on around us.[8]

Thus, it has been argued that some delusions are adaptive not only psychologically, by temporarily reducing anxiety, but also in other ways (Mishara & Corlett, 2009). The suggestion is that delusions allow us to keep in touch with our environment. This claim can be explained by reference to how delusions are adopted. In one influential hypothesis about delusion formation, during the prodromal stage of psychosis, prediction-error signals are produced when there is no real mismatch between prediction and actual inputs. We feel that something significant is happening because our experience does not match our predictions. When this happens, our internal model of the world is thought to be incorrect and undergoes revision. As a result of excessive prediction-error signals, automated and habitual learning is compromised and conscious and controlled processes take over instead.

When the delusion is formed, not only does it put an end to overwhelming anxiety, but it also helps overcome the sense of unpredictability caused by the inaccurate coding of prediction errors. What was experienced as salient is no longer seen as requiring attention, because the delusion can explain it. Thus, the processes underlying automated and habitual learning can resume. This also makes sense of the persistence of delusions. The belief is reinforced every time a new prediction error is registered, given that it has become the default explanation of the unexpected data.

[7] See for instance: "This general delusional atmosphere with all its vagueness of content must be unbearable. Patients obviously suffer terribly under it and to reach some definite idea at last is like being relieved of some enormous burden […] The achievement brings strength and comfort […] No dread is worse than that of danger unknown" (Jaspers, 1963, p. 98).

[8] See for instance: "Delusion formation can be seen as an adaptive process of attributing meaning to experience through which order and security are gained, the novel experience is incorporated within the patient's conceptual framework, and the occult potential of its unknownness is defused" (Roberts, 1992, p. 305).

> The delusions [...] involve a 'reorganization' of the patient's experience to maintain behavioral interaction with the environment despite the underlying disruption to perceptual binding processes [...] At the Aha-moment, the 'shear pin' breaks, or as Conrad puts it, the patient is unable to shift 'reference-frame' to consider the experience from another perspective. The delusion disables flexible, controlled conscious processing from continuing to monitor the mounting distress of the wanton prediction error during delusional mood and thus deters cascading toxicity. At the same time, automatic habitual responses are preserved, possibly even enhanced. (Mishara & Corlett, 2009, p. 531)

We saw in this section that delusions can play an adaptive role, by offering psychological relief from negative emotions and by restoring an epistemically beneficial engagement with reality (Bortolotti, 2016) after the severe disruption due to hypersalience. The consideration of these positive effects prompts us to challenge the claim that epistemically irrational beliefs cannot be good for us.

4.7 "Irrational Beliefs Are the Exception"

We saw that delusions are paradigmatic examples of epistemically irrational beliefs. But not all epistemically rational beliefs are unusual or infrequent. Although the type of delusional belief that attracts the attention of healthcare professionals is relatively rare, beliefs that satisfy the conditions for epistemic rationality and share significant epistemic features with delusions can be easily found in the non-clinical population. The prejudiced belief that members of a certain ethnic group are violent or lazy is not obviously less epistemically irrational than the delusional belief that our neighbor is a spy paid by the government to follow our movements. Superstitious beliefs about nights of full moon causing accidents share many of the epistemic features of delusions: they are badly supported by the available evidence, and they are resistant to counterevidence and counterargument. The reason why prejudiced and superstitious beliefs come across as less puzzling than delusions is that they very widespread and not particularly distressing to those who report them.[9] Here I am going to focus on the literature suggesting that we have a tendency to adopt self-enhancing

[9] See Bortolotti (2009, chapter 3) for a more comprehensive discussion of non-delusional beliefs that are epistemically irrational.

beliefs and make overly optimistic predictions about our future (Jefferson, Bortolotti, & Kuzmanovic, 2017).

Different types of 'positive illusions' are discussed in psychology (Taylor, 1989). We experience the *illusion of control* when we overestimate our capacity to control independent, external events. We think that we have a better chance at winning when we roll the dice in a betting situation. We experience the *better-than-average effect* or have the *illusion of superiority* when we regard ourselves as above average and overrate our performance relative to others in a variety of domains. For instance, many believe that they are above average drivers. The *optimism bias* is a tendency to predict that our future will be largely positive and will yield progress, and that negative events will not be part of our lives. We all underestimate the likelihood of experiencing divorce or developing a serious health condition during our lives.

Are optimistically biased beliefs an instance of irrationality? Here is a reminder that epistemically irrational beliefs can be either true or false, but what makes them irrational is that they are not well supported by the evidence available to us or are insufficiently responsive to new evidence after being adopted. Unrealistically optimistic beliefs fit this description. Often the evidence on which we base our self-related judgements is biased, in that we tend to remember our past successes and forget our failures, or we tend to interpret negative feedback in a positive light. Moreover, we asymmetrically update beliefs about ourselves, taking into account evidence for desirable outcomes but ignoring evidence for undesirable outcomes (Sharot, Korn, & Dolan, 2011). There is an element of motivationally driven distortion of the evidence in the way unrealistically optimistic beliefs are adopted.

To some extent, optimistically biased beliefs can be modified. It has been shown that there are interventions that are at least partially successful in reducing or controlling the extent to which self-related beliefs and predictions are optimistic. For instance, via introspective reflection we can control self-enhancing beliefs at least in the short-term, and self-assessment and predictions about our future are more accurate when we are held accountable for our judgements (Sedikides, Horton, & Gregg, 2007).

Shelley Taylor makes the explicit claim that optimistically biased beliefs are not as fixed as delusional beliefs are, but are flexible and can be adjusted (Taylor, 1989). As we saw, we are known to update our self-related predictions in the light of new evidence, but we tend to do so to a greater extent when the new information is desirable and indicates that our previous estimates were pessimistic. Moreover, we tend to be more optimistic about events that we know we can partially control, and less optimistic just before receiving outcome feedback (Sweeny, Carroll, & Shepperd, 2006). While we may give up our optimistic predictions in order to brace for bad news, we also tend to avoid situations that would cause disappointment, that is, situations in which our optimistic beliefs and predictions could be easily disproved (Armor & Taylor, 1998; Neff & Geers, 2013). Although this is evidence of some flexibility in optimistically biased beliefs, it does not support the claim that we are responsive to evidence in an epistemically rational way when it comes to self-related beliefs and predictions. Rather, the hypothesis is that optimism is strategically enhanced when fewer opportunities for it to be disconfirmed are available.

4.8 Conclusion

Here is what we have learnt from delusions: (1) it is not safe to assume that epistemically irrational beliefs compromise interpretation as it is possible for others to make sense of our behaviour by attributing delusional beliefs to us; (2) it is true that epistemically irrational beliefs can be harmful, and delusions often are very harmful and disruptive, but we should also be open to the possibility that they may have some benefits from a psychological and epistemic point of view, and this might mean that to challenge them is not always the best course of action; (3) epistemically irrational beliefs are not rare and there are many beliefs that share the same epistemic features of delusions but are widespread in the non-clinical population.

Why does all of this matter? Suppose that the attribution of epistemically irrational beliefs contributes to our attempts to explain and predict each other's behaviour, and adopting some of these epistemically irrational beliefs is instrumental to our maintaining some engagement with the surrounding environment in critical situations, irrespective of whether the beliefs are unusual or mundane. Then, there are wide-ranging implications for philosophy, but also for our conception of delusions as symptoms of a mental health issue.

First, as philosophers who intend to gain a better understanding of the workings of the mind, we should be ready to reassess the nature of the links that we identify between core concepts. What is the relationship between rationality and interpretation, rationality and happiness, rationality and knowledge, rationality and success? Such questions have no straight-forward or general answer. We may find it intuitive and coherent with other things that we believe that irrationality leads to the paralysis of interpretation, ignorance, and misery, and in some cases that will happen. But if that is not always the case, then we should get to work and identify the more complex relationships there may be between having beliefs that are ill-grounded and impervious to counterevidence, and the goals we pursue in our lives. In what circumstances is an irrational belief important to us, enabling us to engage successfully with our environment? In what circumstances is it so harmful and disruptive that we should attempt to get rid of it as soon as we can?

Second, it is not obvious that epistemically irrational beliefs should be corrected, challenged, or regarded as a glitch in an otherwise rational belief system. The whole attitude towards such beliefs should change. We all have many epistemically irrational beliefs, and they are not always a sign that we lack credibility or we are mentally unwell. Rather, they are predictable features of human cognition (Puddifoot and Bortolotti, 2018). We are not unbiased in the way we weigh up evidence and we tend to be conservative once we have adopted a belief, making it hard for new contrary evidence to unsettle our existing convictions. Some delusions are just a vivid illustration of a general tendency that is widely shared and hard to counteract. Delusions, just like more common epistemically irrational beliefs, may be a significant obstacle to the achievements of our goals and may cause a rift between our way of seeing the world and other people's way. That is why it is important to develop a critical attitude towards their content. But it would be reckless not to acknowledge that there are situations in which such beliefs have a role to play, maybe allowing us to manage some very strong emotions or to respond to some adverse events that have a dramatic impact on our lives. In such situations, dismissing the belief as a mark of madness may not be the best course of action; at least, not before there is some understanding of how the belief emerged, and what role it has in our mental economy.

The picture I have sketched is a picture of continuity between so-called *normal* and *abnormal* cognition. Irrationality is a feature of normal cognition, and as such it cannot be the criterion of demarcation between beliefs that are 'healthy' and beliefs that are 'pathological'. In recent years, there have been many attempts to explain the pathological nature of delusions, and the general direction of such attempts has been to identify the problem with something other than the epistemic features of the delusional belief. For instance, Miyazono (2015) defends the view that delusions are pathological because they are *harmful dysfunctions*, that is, they are beliefs that negatively affect wellbeing and are caused by mechanisms that do not work properly. According to another account, by Petrolini (2017), the pathological nature of delusions is due to the person losing the capacity for *relevance detection*, that is, the capacity to determine which aspects of the environment are important within a given context.

These are interesting proposals which elucidate some aspects of delusions and deserve further consideration. But here is a more radical suggestion, maybe anticipating a new potential contribution that delusion research could make to the philosophy of the mind. What if there are no *pathological beliefs*? What if the locus of any pathology is the person as a whole? When the person is unwell, then there is a pathological *state* that needs to be addressed in order to restore health. The pathological state can manifest with unusual beliefs, hallucinations, emotional dysregulation, and so on, but such beliefs, experiences, and mood changes are not themselves pathological, as in other circumstances they may not cause any harm. It is in the *context* of what happens to the person as a whole that their role as symptoms can be assessed, and even when they contribute to the pathological state, they may have other roles to play that are either neutral or even positive in some respects.

References

American Psychiatric Association. (2013). *Diagnostic and statistical manual of mental disorders* (5th ed.). Washington, DC: American Psychiatric Association.

Bergstein, M., Weizman, A., & Solomon, Z. (2008). Sense of coherence among delusional patients: Prediction of remission and risk of relapse. *Comprehensive Psychiatry, 49*, 288–296.

Bortolotti, L. (2015). The epistemic innocence of motivated delusions. *Consciousness and Cognition, 33*, 490–499.

Bortolotti, L. (2016). The epistemic benefits of elaborated and systematised delusions in schizophrenia. *British Journal for the Philosophy of Science, 67*(3), 879–900.

Bortolotti, L., & Broome, M. (2012). Affective dimensions of the phenomenon of double bookkeeping in delusions. *Emotion Review, 4*(2), 187–191.

Bortolotti, L., Gunn, R., & Sullivan-Bissett, E. (2016). What makes a belief delusional? In I. Mac Carthy, K. Sellevold, & O. Smith (Eds.), *Cognitive confusions: Dreams, delusions and illusions in early modern culture*. Cambridge, UK: Legenda.

Fulford, K. W., Stanghellini, G., & Broome, M. (2004). What can philosophy do for psychiatry? *World Psychiatry, 3*(3), 130–135.

Gerrans, P. (2000). Refining the explanation of the Cotard's delusion. In M. Coltheart & M. Davies (Eds.), *Pathologies of belief* (pp. 111–122). Oxford, UK: Blackwell.

Gilleen, J., & David, A. S. (2005). The cognitive neuropsychiatry of delusions: From psychopathology to neuropsychology and back again. *Psychological Medicine, 35*, 5–12.

Gunn, R., & Bortolotti, L. (2018). Can delusions play a protective role? *Phenomenology and the Cognitive Sciences, 17*(4), 813–833.

Heal, J. (1998). Understanding other minds from the inside. In A. O'Hear (Ed.), *Current issues in philosophy of mind.* Cambridge, MA: Cambridge University Press.

Jaspers, K. (1963). *General Psychopathology* (7th ed., J. Hoenig & M. W. Hamilton, Trans.). Manchester: Manchester University Press.

Jefferson, A., Bortolotti, L., & Kuzmanovic, B. (2017). What is unrealistic optimism? *Consciousness and Cognition, 50*, 3–11.

Kelly, T. (2003). Epistemic rationality as instrumental rationality: A critique. *Philosophy and Phenomenological Research, 66*, 612–640.

McKay, R., Langdon, R., & Coltheart, M. (2005). "Sleights of mind": Delusions, defences, and self-deception. *Cognitive Neuropsychiatry, 10*, 305–326.

Mishara, A. L. (2010). Klaus Conrad (1905–1961): Delusional mood, psychosis, and beginning schizophrenia. *Schizophrenia Bulletin, 36*, 9–13.

Mishara, A. L., & Corlett, P. (2009). Are delusions biologically adaptive? Salvaging the doxastic shear pin. *Behavioral and Brain Sciences, 32*, 530–531.

Miyazono, K. (2015). Delusions as harmful malfunctioning beliefs. *Consciousness and Cognition, 33*, 561–573.

Petrolini, V. (2017). What makes delusions pathological? *Philosophical Psychology, 30*(4), 502–523.

Puddifoot, K., & Bortolotti, L. (2018). Epistemic innocence and the production of false memory beliefs. *Philosophical Studies*, 1–26.

Roberts, G. (1991). Delusional belief systems and meaning in life: A preferred reality? *The British Journal of Psychiatry, 159*, S19–S28.

Roberts, G. (1992). The origins of delusion. *The British Journal of Psychiatry, 161*, 298–308.

Roberts, G. (2006). Understanding madness. In G. Roberts, S. Davenport, F. Holloway, & T. Tattan (Eds.), *Enabling recovery: The principles and practice of rehabilitation psychiatry* (pp. 93–111). London: Gaskell.

Sharot, T., Korn, C. W., & Dolan, R. J. (2011). How unrealistic optimism is maintained in the face of reality. *Nature Neuroscience, 14*, 1475–1479.

Taylor, S. E. (1989). *Positive illusions: Creative self-deception and the healthy mind.* New York: Basic Books.

BY

Index[1]

A

B

[1] Note: Page numbers followed by 'n' refer to notes.

L. Bortolotti (ed.), *Delusions in Context*,
https://doi.org/10.1007/978-3-319-97202-2

Lightning Source UK Ltd.
Milton Keynes UK
UKHW02n0649101018
330306UK00019B/464/P

9 783319 972015